Signals

Signals

Evolution, Learning, & Information

Brian Skyrms

OXFORD
UNIVERSITY PRESS

OXFORD

UNIVERSITY PRESS

Great Clarendon Street, Oxford OX2 6DP
United Kingdom

Oxford University Press is a department of the University of Oxford.
It furthers the University's objective of excellence in research, scholarship,
and education by publishing worldwide. Oxford is a registered trade mark of
Oxford University Press in the UK and in certain other countries

British Library Cataloguing in Publication Data
Data available

Library of Congress Cataloging in Publication Data
Data available

ISBN 978-0-19-958294-5

For Pauline, Michael, and Gabriel

Acknowledgments

This book grew out of my 2006 Presidential address to the Philosophy of Science Association, and the research was partially supported by air force grant FA9550-08-1-0389. Many friends and colleagues contributed to the results presented here. Fundamental analyses of evolutionary dynamics applied to signaling are due to Josef Hofbauer and Simon Huttegger. The basic result for learning dynamics is due to Raffaele Argiento, Robin Pemantle, and Stanislav Volkov. Jeffrey Barrett invented a model in which individuals simultaneously invent categories and code. Kevin Zollman, Rory Smead, and Elliott Wagner provided important results about learning and networks. Jason McKenzie Alexander suggested an interesting version of forgetting to augment learning dynamics. Carl Bergstrom, Michael Lachmann, and Matina Donaldson analyze the equilibrium structure of situations in which there are too few signals. Sven Lauer saw clearly the relation between my version of informational content and the standard philosopher's notion of a proposition. Simon Huttegger showed how inductive reasoners can learn to form an information ring. Sandy Zabell introduced me to Hoppe's urn, which is the key to a model of inventing new signals.

I owe a lot to feedback that I received from participants in seminars at Stanford and the University of California, Irvine. Duncan Luce read the entire manuscript and provided valuable comments. I would also like to thank Peter Godfrey-Smith, Fred Dretske, Patrick Grim, Louis Narens, Natalia Komarova, Kimberly Jameson, Don Saari, Ken Binmore, Ed Hopkins, Larry Samuelson Simon Levin, Steve Frank, and Patrick Suppes for discussions.

Contents

Introduction

"The word is the shadow of the deed."
Democritus

In a famous essay on meaning, H. Paul Grice distinguished between *natural* and *non-natural* meaning. Natural meaning depends on associations arising from natural processes. I say that all meaning is natural meaning.[1] This is in the tradition of Democritus, Aristotle, Adam Smith, and David Hume, Darwin, Bertrand Russell, and Ludwig Wittgenstein, David Lewis, and Ruth Millikan. It is opposed to Platonism, Cartesianism, and various stripes of *geistphilosophy*.

Can the meaning of words arise spontaneously, by chance? We begin by attacking the question (at a high level of abstraction) with a combination of modern tools. The first is the theory of signaling games, in whose use we follow the philosopher David Lewis. The second is the mathematical theory of information, where we replace rather ill-defined questions about the meaning of words with clearer questions about the information carried by signals. This uses ideas deriving ultimately from the theory of Claude Shannon, but elaborated by Solomon Kullback in such a way as to provide a natural definition of the *quantity* of information in a signal. One of the original contributions of this book is a natural definition of the informational *content* in a signal that generalizes philosophers' notion of a proposition as a set of possible worlds. The third consists in the Darwinian idea of evolution by differential reproduction and natural variation. In particular, we use models of replicator dynamics. The fourth consists of theories of trial and error learning. The evolutionary question is

---

[1] Grice is pointing to a real distinction, but in my view it is the distinction between conventional and non-conventional meaning. Conventional meaning is a variety of natural meaning. Natural dynamic processes—evolution and learning—create conventions.

re-posed as a learning question. Can signals spontaneously acquire information through naive learning in repeated interaction? The story, even at this simplified abstract level, is much richer than you might expect. At a more concrete level, there is a vast and growing scientific literature on signaling in and between cells, neurology, animal signaling, and human signaling, that we cannot hope to address here. An account of the biochemistry of signaling in one bacterium *Myxococcus xanthus*, if it were fully known, would take a book of its own—and I would not be the person to write it. I will stick to the abstract, game-theoretic level. At that level of analysis there is one basic point that is clear: Democritus was right.

Is this the end of our story? No, it is the beginning. Signaling systems grow. That means that signaling games themselves evolve. They are not fixed, closed interaction structures but rather open structures capable of change. We need to study mechanisms that can account for such change. There are two stages of this process that are addressed in this book. One is the invention of new signals. The invention of the original signals needed to get signaling off the ground is a case in point, but there is also the case of invention to get out of information bottlenecks. This book introduces a new account—a new mathematical model—of learning with invention. Invention completely alters the dynamics of learning in signaling situations. The second stage consists in the juxtaposition of simple signals to produce complex signals. Complex signals are a great advance in the evolution of signaling systems. Humans are, of course, very good at this. But, contrary to some claims, neither syntax nor complex signals are the exclusive preserve of humans. It is best then, to think of these not as the results of some evolutionary miracle, but rather as the natural product of some gradual process.

Signaling transmits information, but it does far more than this. To see this we need to move further than the simple signaling games with one sender and one receiver. Signals operate in networks of senders and receivers at all levels of life. Information is transmitted, but it is also processed in various ways. Among other things, that is how we *think*—just signals running around a very complicated signaling network. Very simple signaling systems should be able to learn to implement very simple information processing tasks by very simple means, and indeed they can.

Signaling networks also give a richer view of a dual aspect of signals. Signals inform action, and signaling networks co-ordinate action. Signaling is a key ingredient in the evolution of teamwork. You can think of the flow of information in a corporation, or a government, or a publisher. But you can also think of teamwork in animals, in cooperative hunting, cooperative breeding, cooperative defense against predators, and cooperative construction of living spaces. These kinds of teamwork are found not only in mammals, birds, and the insect societies, but also more recently in micro-organisms. Teamwork is found in bacteria (*Myxococcus*), amoeboids (cellular slime molds), and algae (*Volvox*). These organisms are models of the transition from unicellular organisms to multicellularity. And the internal workings of multicellular organisms are themselves marvels of teamwork. The coordination of the parts in each of these cases is effected by signals. Of course, in any complex organization, information transmission and processing and coordination of action may not be entirely separate. Rather, they might be thought of as different aspects of the flow of information.

Signaling may evolve for various purposes in networks with different structures. We look only at simple structures that can be thought of as building blocks for larger, more complex networks. But even at the level of such simple network structures, we have to think of the network topology itself evolving. The last chapter of this book gives a brief introduction to this field, and introduces novel low-rationality payoff-based dynamics that learns to network just as well as higher-rationality best-response dynamics.

What is the relation of signaling theory to philosophy? It is epistemology, because it deals with selection, transmission, and processing of information. It is philosophy of (proto)-language. It addresses cooperation and collective action—issues that usually reside in social and political philosophy. It does not quite fit into any of these categories, and gives each a somewhat novel slant. That's good, because the theory of signaling is full of fascinating unexplored questions.

1

Signals

> "Two savages, who had never been taught to speak, but had been brought up remote from the societies of men, would naturally begin to form that language by which they would endeavor to make their mutual wants intelligible to each other..."
>
> Adam Smith, *Considerations Concerning the First Formation of Languages*

What is the origin of signaling systems? Adam Smith suggests that there is nothing mysterious about it. Two perfectly ordinary people who did not have a signaling system would naturally invent one. In the first century BC, Vitruvius says much the same thing:

In that time of men when utterance of a sound was purely individual, from daily habits they fixed on articulate words just as they happened to come; then, from indicating by name things in common use, the result was in this chance way they began to talk, and thus originated conversation with one another.

Vitruvius is echoing the view of the great atomist Democritus, who lived four centuries earlier. Democritus held that signals were conventional and that they arose by chance.[1] Can it be true? If so, *how* can it be true?

---

[1] Another echo is to be found in Diodorus of Sicily:

"The sounds they made had no sense and were confused; but gradually they articulated their expressions, and by establishing symbols among themselves for every sort of object they came to express themselves on all matters in a way intelligible to one another. Such groups

The leading alternative view was that some signals, at least originally, had their meaning "by nature"—that is, that there was an innate signaling system.[2] At the time this may have seemed like an acceptable explanation, but after Darwin, we must say that it is no explanation at all. Bare postulation of an evolutionary miracle is no more explanatory than postulation of a miraculous invention. Either way, some work needs to be done.

Whatever one thinks of human signals, it must be acknowledged that information is transmitted by signaling systems at all levels of biological organization. Monkeys,[3] birds,[4] bees, and even bacteria[5] have signaling systems. Multicellular organisms are only possible because internal signals coordinate the actions of their constituents. We will survey some of the signaling systems in nature in Chapter 2. Some of these signaling systems are innate in the strongest sense. Some are not.

We now have not one but two questions: *How can interacting individuals spontaneously learn to signal? How can species spontaneously evolve signaling systems?*

I would like to indicate how we can bring contemporary theoretical tools to bear on these questions.

came into existence throughout the inhabited world, and not all men had the same language, since each group organized their expressions as chance had it."

Translation from Barnes 2001: 221.
See also Verlinski 2005 and Barnes 2001: 223. Proclus says:

"Both Pythagoras and Epicurus were of Cratylus' opinion. Democritus and Aristotle were of Hermongenes" (5,2526).

and:

"Democritus who said that names are conventional formulated this principle in four dialectical proofs... Therefore names are arbitrary, not natural." (6,207,1)

Translation from Duvick 2007.

[2] I am, of necessity, drastically oversimplifying the ancient debate here. See van den Berg 2008.

[3] Cheney and Seyfarth 1990.

[4] See Charrier and Sturdy 2005 for an avian signaling system with syntactical rules, and Marler 1999 for shadings of "innateness" in sparrow songs.

[5] See the review article of Taga and Bassler 2003.

Sender-receiver

In 1969 David Lewis framed the problem in a clean and simple way by introducing sender-receiver games.[6] There are two players, the sender and the receiver. Nature chooses a state at random and the sender observes the state chosen. The sender then sends a signal to the receiver, who cannot observe the state directly but does observe the signal. The receiver then chooses an act, the outcome of which affects them both, with the payoff depending on the state. Both have pure common interest—they get the same payoff—and there is exactly one "correct" act for each state. In the correct act-state combination they both get positive payoff; otherwise payoff is zero. The simplest case is one where there are the same number of states, acts, and signals. This is where we will begin.

Signals are not endowed with any intrinsic meaning. If they are to acquire meaning, the players must somehow find their way to information transmission. Lewis confines his analysis to equilibria of the game, although more generally we would want to investigate information transmission out of equilibrium as well. When transmission is perfect, so that the act always matches the state and the payoff is optimal, Lewis calls the equilibrium a *signaling system*. It is a virtue of Lewis's formulation that we do not have to endow the sender and receiver with a pre-existing mental language in order to define a signaling system.

That is not to say that mental language is precluded. The state that the sender observes might be "What I want to communicate" and the receiver's act might be concluding "Oh, she intended to communicate that." Accounts framed in terms of mental language,[7] or ideas or intentions can fit perfectly well within sender-receiver games. But the framework also accommodates signaling where no plausible account of mental life is available.

---

[6] Russell 1921 is a precursor to Lewis. In an important paper, Crawford and Sobel 1982 analyze a model that generalizes signaling games in a different direction from that pursued here.

[7] Such as Hurford 1989 and Komarova, Niyogi, and Nowak 2001.

If we start with a pair of sender and receiver strategies, and switch the messages around the same way in both, we get the same payoffs. In particular, permutation of messages takes one signaling-system equilibrium into another. This fundamental symmetry is what makes Lewis signaling games a model in which the meaning of signals is *purely conventional*.[8] It also raises in stark form a question that bothered some philosophers from ancient times onward. There seems to be no *sufficient reason* why one signaling system rather than another should evolve. Of course, there may be many signaling systems in nature which got an initial boost from some sort of natural salience. But it is worth considering, with Lewis, the worst case scenario in which natural salience is absent and signaling systems are purely conventional.

Information in signals

Signals carry information.[9] The natural way to measure the information in a signal is to measure the extent that the use of that particular signal changes probabilities.[10] Accordingly, there are two kinds of information in the signals in Lewis sender-receiver games: information about what state the sender has observed and information about what act the receiver will take. The first kind of information measures effectiveness of the sender's use of signals to discriminate states; the second kind measures the effectiveness of the signal in changing the receiver's probabilities of action.[11]

---

[8] Some signaling interactions may not have this strong symmetry and then signals may not be perfectly conventional. There may be some natural salience for a particular signaling system. Here we are addressing the worst case for the spontaneous emergence of signaling.

[9] I follow Dretske 1981 in taking the transmission of information as one of the fundamental issues of epistemology.

[10] This can be measured in a principled way using the discrimination information of Kullback and Leibler 1951; Kullback 1959. We will look at this more closely in Chapter 3.

[11] Corresponding to these two types of information, we can talk about two types of content of a signal. See Russell 1921; Millikan 1984; Harms 2004.

Both kinds of information are maximal in a signaling-system equilibrium. But this does not uniquely characterize a signaling system. Both kinds of information can also be maximal in a state in which the players *mis*coordinate, and the receiver always does an act that is wrong for the state. Then there is plenty of information of both kinds, but it seems natural to say that information has not been successfully *transmitted* (or perhaps that *mis*information is transmitted.)

Transmission of information clearly consists of more than the quantity of information in the signal. To deal with this example, you might think that we have to build in mentalistic concept of information—specifying what the sender *intended* the signal to mean and what the receiver took it to mean. Within the framework of Lewis signaling games this is not necessary. Sender and receiver have pure common interest. Perfect information about the state is transmitted perfectly if the receiver acts just as he would if he had direct knowledge of the state. As Democritus said, "The word is the shadow of the act."[12]

A general treatment of information in signaling requires a lot more than this simple observation. In Chapter 3, I will develop a unified framework for both *informational quantity* and *informational content* of signals. The notion of informational content will be new, and will allow a resolution of some philosophical puzzles.

Evolution

As a simple explicit model of evolution, we start with the *replicator dynamics*.[13] This has interpretations both for genetic evolution and for cultural evolution. The population is large, and either differential reproduction or differential imitation lead the population proportion of strategy A, p (A), to change as:

---

[12] Barnes 1982: 468.
[13] For a canonical reference, see Hofbauer and Sigmund 1998.

$$dp(A)/dt = p(A)[U(A) - U]$$

where $U(A)$ is the average payoff to strategy A and U is the average payoff in the population.

Evolutionary dynamics could operate on one population of senders and another of receivers as in some cases of interspecies communication, or it could operate on a single population, where individuals sometimes find themselves in the role of sender and sometimes in the role of receiver.

Consider the two-population model for the simplest Lewis signaling game—two states, two signals, two acts. Nature chooses a state by flipping a fair coin. And for further simplification, suppose the population has senders who only send different signals for different states and receivers who only perform different acts when they get different signals. There are then only two sender's strategies:

S1: State 1 => Signal 1
    State 2 => Signal 2
S2: State 1 => Signal 2
    State 2 => Signal 1

and only two receiver's strategies:

R1: Signal 1 => Act 1
    Signal 2 => Act 2
R2: Signal 1 => Act 2
    Signal 2 => Act 1

The pairs <S1,R1> and <S2,R2> are the signaling system equilibria. (We will consider varying the numbers of states, signals and acts, and the probabilities of the states, and the payoffs in subsequent chapters.)

The population dynamics lives on a square, with p(S2), the proportion of senders playing strategy S2, on the y axis and p(R2), the proportion of receivers playing strategy R2, on the x axis. It looks like this:

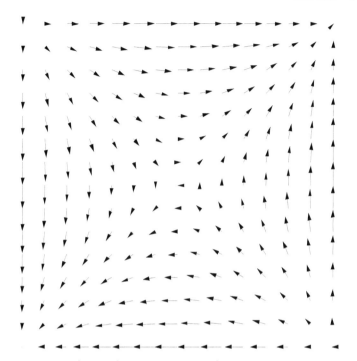

Figure 1.1: Replicator dynamics, two populations.

There are 5 dynamic equilibria—the four corners and one in the center of the square—but three of them are dynamically unstable. The two signaling systems are the only stable equilibria, and evolution carries almost every state of the combination of populations to either one signaling system or another.

Consider a one-population model where the agent's contingency plans, *if sender . . . and if receiver . . .* correspond to the four corners of the model we just considered. The dynamics lives on a tetrahedron. It looks like this:

The vertices are dynamic equilibria, and in addition there is a line of equilibria running through the center of the tetrahedron. But again, all the equilibria are unstable except for the signaling systems. All states to one side of a plane cutting through the tetrahedron are carried to one signaling system; all to the other side to the other signaling system.

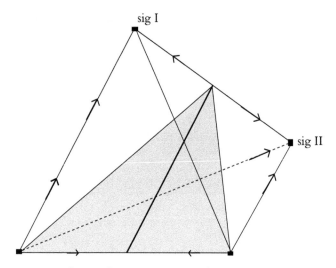

Figure 1.2: Replicator dynamics, one population.

Almost every possible state of the population is carried to a signaling system. More complex cases are discussed in Chapters 4 and 5.

We see in these simple cases how a perfectly symmetric model can be expected to yield an asymmetric outcome. In our two examples, the principle of sufficient reason is defeated by *symmetry breaking* in the evolutionary dynamics. The population moves to a signaling system as if—one might say—guided by an unseen hand.

Learning strategies

As a simple explicit model of unsophisticated learning, we start with reinforcement according to Richard Herrnstein's *matching law*—the probability of choosing an action is proportional to its accumulated rewards.[14] We start with some initial weights, perhaps equal,

---

[14] First proposed in Herrnstein 1970 as a quantification of Thorndike's law of effect, later used by Roth and Erev 1995 to model experimental human data on learning in games, by Othmer and Stevens 1997 to model chemotaxis in social bacteria, and by Skyrms and Pemantle 2000 to model social network formation.

assigned to each action. An act is chosen with probability proportional to its weight. The payoff gained is added to the weight for the act that was chosen, and the process repeats. As the weights build up, the process slows down in accordance with what psychologists call the law of practice.

Consider repeated interactions between two individuals, one sender and one receiver, who learn strategies by this kind of reinforcement. This set-up resembles the two-population evolutionary model, except that the process is not deterministic, but chancy. For a nice tractable example consider the two-state, two-signal, two-act signaling game of the last section. Computer simulations show agents always learning to signal, and learning is reasonably fast.

Learning actions

We helped the emergence of signaling in the foregoing model by letting reinforcement work on *complete strategies* in the signaling game—on functions from input to output. Essentially, the modeler has done some of the work for the learners. I take this as contrary to the spirit of Democritus, according to which the learners should not have to conceive of the problem strategically. Let us reconceptualize the problem by having reinforcement work on *single actions* and see if we still get the same result.

To implement this for the simplest Lewis signaling game, the sender has separate reinforcements for each state. You can think of it as an urn for state 1, with red balls for signal 1 and black balls for signal 2; and another such urn for state 2. The receiver also has two urns, one for each signal received, and each containing balls for the two acts. Nature flips a fair coin to choose the state. The sender observes the state and draws a ball from the corresponding urn to choose a signal. The receiver observes the signal and draws a ball from the corresponding urn to choose an act. The act is either successful, in being the act that pays off in that state, or not. Reinforcement for a successful act is like adding a ball of the color drawn to the sender and receiver urn just sampled. The individuals are being reinforced for "what to do on this sort of occasion." We can then ask what happens when these occasions fit together to form a signaling game.

This model appears to be more challenging than the one in the previous section. There are now four interacting reinforcement processes instead of two. Equilibria where the sender ignores the state and the receiver ignores the signal are no longer ruled out by appeal to the agents' intelligence and good intentions. Nevertheless, there is now an analytic proof[15] that reinforcement learning converges to a signaling system with probability one. The robustness of this result over a range of learning rules is discussed in Chapters 6 and 7.

States, acts, and signals

In the simplest Lewis signaling games, the number of states, acts, and signals are assumed to be the same. Why should this be so? What if there is a mismatch? There may be extra signals, or too few signals, or not enough acts. All these possibilities raise questions that are interesting both philosophically and mathematically.

Suppose there are too many signals. Do synonyms persist, or do some signals fall out of use until only the number required to identify the states remain in use? Suppose there are too few signals. Then there is, of necessity, an information bottleneck. Does efficient signaling evolve; do the players learn to do as well as possible? Suppose there are lots of states, but not many acts. How do the acts affect how the signaling system partitions the states?

If we have two states, two acts and three signals, we could imagine that the third signal gets in the way of efficient signaling, or that one signal falls out of use and one ends up with essentially a two-signal system, or that one signal comes to stand for one state and the other two persist as synonyms for the other state. Simulations of the

[15]   Argiento, Pemantle, Skyrms, and Volkov 2009.

learning process of the last section always produce efficient signaling, often with the persistence of synonyms. Learning is about as fast as in the case where there are only two signals.

If we have three states, three acts and only two signals, there is an information bottleneck. The best that the players could do is to get it right ⅔ of the time. This could be managed in various ways. The sender might use signals deterministically to partition the states—for example, send signal 1 in state 1 and signal 2 otherwise. An optimal receiver's strategy in reply would be to do act 1 when receiving signal 1, and to randomize between acts 2 and 3 with any probability. This identifies a whole line of equilibria, corresponding to the randomizing probability. Alternatively, the receiver could be deterministic—for example, doing act 1 for signal 1 and act 2 for signal 2. If so, an optimal sender's strategy to pair with this would always do sending signal 1 in state 1 and signal 2 in state 2, but randomizing in state 3. This identifies another line of efficient equilibria.[16] There are, of course, also lots of inefficient equilibria. Simulations always deliver efficient equilibria. They are always of the first kind, not the second. That is to say the signaling system always partitions the states. Learning is still fast.

If we have three states, but only two signals and two acts, we can have act 1 right for state 1, and act 2 right for state 3, and then vary the payoffs for state 2:

Payoffs	State 1	State 2	State 3
Act 1	1	1−e	0
Act 2	0	e	1

If e < .5 it is best to have one signal (which elicits act 1) sent in both state 1 and state 2; and the other signal (which elicits act 2) sent in state 3. If e > .5 an efficient equilibrium lumps states 2 and 3 together. The optimal payoff possible depends on e: ⅔ for e = .5 and 1 for e = 0 or e = 1. For the whole range of values, optimal

---

[16] Notice that these two lines share a point. If we consider all the lines of efficient equilibria, we have a cycle.

signaling emerges. These generalized signaling games are discussed in Chapter 8. The signaling game itself may not be fixed. The game structure itself may evolve. A model of signaling with invention of new signals is introduced in Chapter 9. The combination of simple signals to form complex signals is discussed in Chapter 11.

Signaling networks

Signaling is not restricted to the simple 1-sender, 1-receiver case discussed so far. Alarm calls usually involve one sender and many receivers, perhaps with some of the receivers being eavesdroppers from other species. Quorum signaling in bacteria has many individuals playing the role of both sender and receiver. The brain continually receives and dispatches multiple signals, as do many of its constituents. Most natural signaling occurs in networks. A signaling network can be thought of as a directed graph, with an edge directed from node A to node B signifying that A sends signals to B. All our examples so far have been instantiations of the simplest possible case; one sender sends signals to one receiver.

There are other simple topologies that are of interest. One that I discussed elsewhere[17] involved multiple senders and one receiver. I imagined two senders who observed different partitions of the possible states.

In the context of alarm calls, if one sender observes a snake or leopard is present, and another observes that there is no snake, a receiving monkey might be well advised to take the action appropriate to evade a leopard. Multiple senders who transmit different information leave the receiver with a problem of logical inference.

---

[17] Skyrms 2000, 2004.

It is not simply the problem of drawing a correct inference, but rather the problem of drawing the correct inference relevant to his decision problem. For instance, suppose sender 1 observes the truth value of p and then sends signal A or signal B, and sender 2 observes the truth value of q and sends C or D. Maximum specificity is required where the receiver has four acts, one right for each combination of truth values. But a different decision problem might require the receiver to compute the truth value (p exclusive or q) and to do one act if true and another if false.

Senders may observe different aspects of nature by chance, but they might also be able to choose what they observe. Nature may present receivers with different decision problems. Thus, a receiver might be in a situation where he would like to ask a sender to make the right observation. This calls for a dialogue, where information flows in both directions.

●↔●

Nature flips a coin and presents player 2 with one or another decision problem. Player 2 sends one of two signals to player 1. Player 1 selects one of two partitions of the state of nature to observe. Nature flips a coin and presents player 1 with the true state. Player 1 sends one of two signals to player 2. Player 2 chooses one of two acts. Here a question and answer signaling system can guarantee that player 2 always does the right thing.

A sender may distribute information to several receivers.

●←●→●

One instance is the case of eavesdropping, where a third individual listens in to a two-person sender-receiver game, with the act of the third person having payoff consequences for himself, but not for the other two.[18] In a somewhat more demanding setup, the sender sends separate signals to multiple receivers who then have to

---

[18] There are also more complicated forms of eavesdropping, where the third party's actions have consequences for the signalers and there is conflict of interest. For a fascinating instance, where plants eavesdrop on bacteria, see Bauer and Mathesius 2004.

perform complementary acts for everyone to get paid. For instance, each receiver must choose one of two acts, and the sender observes one of four states of nature and sends one of two signals to each receiver. Each combination of acts pays off in exactly one state.

Signalers may form chains, where information is passed along.

In one scenario, the first individual observes the state and signals the state, and the second observes the signal and signals the third, which must perform the right act to ensure a common payoff. There is no requirement that the second individual sends the same signal that she receives. She might function as a translator from one signaling system to another.

When we extend the basic Lewis game to each of these networks, computer simulations show reinforcement learning converging to signaling systems—although a full mathematical analysis of these cases remains to be done. It is remarkable that such an unsophisticated form of learning can arrive at optimal solutions to these various problems. Simple signaling networks are discussed as a locus of information processing in Chapter 10 and as a component of teamwork in Chapter 13.

These networks are the simplest examples of large classes on phenomena of general interest. They also can be thought of as modules, which appear as constituents of more complex and interesting networks that process and transmit information. It is possible for modules to be learned in simple signaling interactions, and then assembled into complex networks by either reinforcement or some more sophisticated form of learning. The analogous process operates in evolution. The dynamics of formation of a simple signaling network is discussed in Chapter 14.

Conclusion

How do these results generalize? This is not so much a single question as an invitation to explore an emerging field. Even the simplest extensions of the models I have shown here are full of surprising and interesting phenomena. We have seen the importance of focusing on adaptive dynamics. The dynamics can be varied. On the evolutionary side, we can add mutation to differential reproduction. In addition, we might move from the large population, deterministic model of the replicator dynamics to a small population stochastic model. The mathematical structure of one natural stochastic model of differential reproduction is remarkably similar to our model of reinforcement learning.[19] On the learning side, we should also consider more sophisticated types of learning. From considering evolution in a fixed signaling game we might move to evolution of the game structure itself. We should explore both signaling on various kinds of networks, but also the dynamics of formation of signaling networks. The rest of this book is an introduction to these topics.

We started with a fundamental question. Suppose we start without pre-existing meaning. Is it possible that, under favorable conditions, unsophisticated learning dynamics can spontaneously generate meaningful signaling? The answer is affirmative. The parallel question for evolution turns out to be not so different, and is answered in the same way. The adaptive dynamics achieves meaning by breaking symmetry. Democritus was right. It remains to explore all the ways in which he was right.

---

[19] Schreiber 2001.

2

Signals in Nature

> *"Since monkeys certainly understand much that is said to them by man, and when wild, utter signal-cries of danger to their fellows; and since fowls give distinct warnings for danger on the ground, or in the sky from hawks (both, as well, as third cry, intelligible to dogs), may not some unusually wise ape-like animal have imitated the growl of a beast of prey, and thus told his fellow-monkeys the nature of the expected danger? This would have been the first step in the formation of a language."*

> Charles Darwin, *The Descent of Man*

Darwin sees some kind of *natural salience* operating at the origin of language. At that point signals are not conventional, but rather the signal is somehow naturally suited to convey its content. Signaling is then gradually modified by evolution. Darwin is thinking of biological evolution, but for humans (and some other species) there is a version of the account that substitutes cultural evolution or social learning for biological evolution. This view of the origins of language goes back to the late Epicureans.[1] They could not see how language could have originated out of nothing by pure convention, because some pre-existing language seems to be required to set up the convention.

The same objection to a kind of conventionalism comes down through the history of philosophy, through Rousseau[2] to Quine's

---

[1] Verlinski 2005.

[2] "a unanimous agreement would have to be proposed, which means that speech seems absolutely necessary to establish the use of speech." *Discourse on Inequality* 94.

"Truth by Convention." It is most trenchantly put by Russell:[3] "We can hardly suppose a parliament of hitherto speechless elders meeting together and agreeing to call a cow a cow and a wolf a wolf."

The conventionalist being refuted is, however, a kind of straw man. That convention need not be explicitly proposed and accepted, but can arise by a gradual evolutionary process, was clearly seen by David Hume:

Two men, who pull the oars of a boat, do it by an agreement or convention, tho' they have never given promises to each other. Nor is the rule concerning the stability of possession the less derive'd from human conventions, that it arises gradually, and acquires force by a slow progression, and. by our repeated experience of the inconveniences of transgressing it. . . . In like manner are languages gradually establish'd by human conventions without any promise.[4]

Hume did not, however, tell us how this process of cultural evolution started in the first place. The possibility of symmetry-breaking, as discussed in Chapter 1, demonstrates the possibility of an origin of signals without any natural salience whatsoever.

In some cases there may well be natural salience, in which case the amplification of pre-existing inclinations into a full fledged signaling system is that much easier. A dog's baring of teeth as a threat gesture is a particularly plausible example. "Bare teeth to bite" leads to "Conspicuously bare teeth to signal on the verge of biting." (But remember that *we* bare our teeth to smile.)

The Darwin–Lucretius scenario of some small initial natural salience amplified by evolutionary feedback may well be the correct one for many evolutionary histories. It does not require any modification of the signaling games introduced in Chapter 1. It can be represented in signaling games simply by moving the initial probabilities off exact symmetry—in a given state the sender is initially more likely to send one particular signal rather than others, and a

---

[3] *The Analysis of Mind*, Lecture X, 113.
[4] Hume, Bk III, Part I, Sec. 2.

receiver is more likely to react to that signal in the appropriate way. That is to say that signaling game models easily accommodate natural salience but do not require it. Democritus' deep insight is fundamental. Even without natural salience, signaling systems can evolve.

There is more in this remarkable passage from Darwin. He already knows about predator-specific alarm calls. A sentinel of the prey species gives an alarm call that not only signals danger, but also identifies the class of predator present. Classes of predators are grouped according to appropriate escape behavior, and a distinct signal is assigned to each. These have recently become well known through the study of Vervet monkeys in the Amboseli forest by Dorothy Cheney and Richard Seyfarth.[5] Subsequently, species-specific alarm calls have been found in many species of monkeys—Diana Monkeys[6] and Campbell's Monkeys[7] in the old world, and two species of Tamarins[8] in the new—as well as in lemurs,[9] a social mongoose,[10] prairie dogs,[11] and red squirrels.[12] A whole series of careful studies shows that they are used by domestic chickens,[13] [14] just as Darwin says they are.

Cheney and Seyfarth[15] show that vervets have distinct alarm calls for different classes of predator: a "cough" for an eagle, a "bark" for a leopard, and a "chutter" for a snake. For each predator a different evasive action is optimal. For leopards it is usually best to run up a tree and out on a branch where a leopard cannot follow; for snakes one should stand tall and scan the ground to locate the snake and then move away from it; for eagles it is best to exit a tree, take cover

[5] Cheney and Seyfarth 1990.
[6] Zuberbühler 2000.
[7] Zuberbühler 2001.
[8] Kirchhof and Hammerschmidt 2006.
[9] Macedonia 1990.
[10] Manser et al. 2002.
[11] Slobodchikoff et al. 1991.
[12] Green and Maegner 1998.
[13] Gyger et al. 1987.
[14] Evans et al. 1994.
[15] Following earlier work by Struhsaker 1967.

in the underbrush, and look upward to detect the location of the predator. Each alarm call elicits the appropriate behavior—both in the natural setting and in experiments where recorded alarm calls are played back.

Nature has presented vervets with something very close to a classic Lewis signaling game and they have achieved something very close to a signaling-system equilibrium. The states are *eagle present*, *leopard present*, *snake present* and the acts are *hide in underbrush, run up tree, scan and move away*. The signaling system consists of a pairing of sender and receiver strategies:

SENDER	RECEIVER
eagle =>cough	*cough=>underbrush*
leopard => bark	*bark=>run up tree*
snake => chutter	*chutter=> scan and move*

that constitutes a Lewis signaling system.

This is, of course a simplification. We could have a state where no predator is present, a null signal consisting of normal sounds, a null action of business as usual, with perhaps some costs to sending a signal other than the null signal. We could include minor predators and minor predator alarm calls, which do really exist. If a leopard is close, a monkey far from a tree might just dive into underbrush. But, for the moment, the idealization is not bad.

The same pattern is repeated in other species with predator-specific alarm calls. Meerkats live in semi-desert areas in South Africa. They are prey to jackals, to eagles and hawks, and to snakes—cape cobra, puff adder, and mole snake. Meerkat alarm calls distinguish these three classes of predator. But they also distinguish the urgency of the threat. This has important implications because of the terrain, and because the meerkats live in burrows and forage within 100–150 feet of a burrow. A high-urgency eagle alarm call will lead meerkats to crouch and freeze. But on hearing a low-urgency eagle alarm call they will run to the nearest burrow and disappear down it.[16]

Darwin notes in passing that one species may understand the signals of another. Vervet monkeys can learn to understand the alarm calls of a bird, the Superb Starling.[17] These birds also produce different alarm calls for aerial and terrestrial predators. When the Superb Starling alarm calls were played back to captive vervets, they took the appropriate evasive action for the indicated type of predator.[18]

This may not be very surprising. Monkeys are very clever. But some birds reciprocate by using the information in alarm calls of monkeys. Diana monkeys in West Africa are prey to leopards and crowned eagles and have distinct alarm calls for each predator. Crowned eagles also prey upon the yellow-casqued hornbill, a large bird about the same size as a Diana monkey, but leopards do not. Playbacks of recorded Diana monkey alarm calls show hornbills responding to Diana monkey eagle alarms calls just as to recorded eagle shrieks, but not to Diana leopard alarm calls and not to leopard growls.[19]

These cases suggest more complex signaling games. The Diana monkeys play the roles of sender and receiver, as in classic Lewis signaling games, but there is also an eavesdropper—the hornbill— who can utilize and benefit from the information in the signal, but whose correct action benefits neither the sender nor receiver. If so, evolution (or learning) of the signaling system is driven by the interaction between the sender and primary receiver, with the eavesdropper learning to get a free ride.

Receiver ← Sender → Eavesdropper

This case offers no difficulties for the evolution of signaling.

---

[16] Manser et al. 2002.

[17] Hauser 1988.

[18] Seyfarth and Cheney 1990.

[19] Rainey et al. 2004.

There are further variations worth considering. The hornbill, when alerted to an aerial predator, may take up the cry and utter its own loud alarm, in which case the monkeys may gain some benefit after all—the hornbill acting as an amplifier of the alarm. On the other hand, there is the case where the predator itself is the third party. The kind of predator who hunts by stealth may be deterred by learning that it has been detected, but a different, swift, predator might be guided to the caller.

The latter case would be an instance of evolution of altruism, and thus strictly speaking not a Lewis signaling game. Such signaling would call for a version of one of the existing evolutionary accounts of evolution of altruism. For instance, altruism may evolve by kin selection. An individual giving the alarm call may expose itself to more danger but nevertheless promote the transmission of the altruistic gene—which is present in kin—by increasing the survival of kin. Where this explanation is correct, one would expect the alarm calls to be given in the presence of kin but neither in solitude, nor in the exclusive presence of strangers. There is evidence that this is often the case.[20] Here, one way of viewing the account is to say that taking account of inclusive fitness, we have a Lewis signaling game after all.[21]

So far, we have dealt with signals that are essentially one-word sentences. That is fine, if there is not much that needs saying. But for a species that needs to communicate a lot of information, this is obviously grossly inefficient. It would be better to be able to construct a variety of complex signals from a small number of simple constituents. We can do it. Can any other species do so?

It is known that non-human primates can be trained to combine symbols to form simple sentences, to construct novel sentences, and

---

[20] Cheney and Seyfarth 1990; Snowdon 1990: 232.

[21] Other accounts of the evolution of altruism, such as direct or indirect reciprocity, could also come into play in giving risky alarm calls. All explanations for the evolution of altruism work by establishing some kind of correlation of types. Such correlation allows a unified treatment of altruistic signaling. See the discussion of "Signals for Altruists" in Skyrms 1996: 94–8.

to use these sentences to communicate. The most remarkable case is that of Kanzi, a Bonobo, whose (adoptive) mother was being trained to use language. Mom was never very good at it, but Kanzi, who was a bystander—not being trained at all—spontaneously picked it up.[22] The "language" consists of lexograms—geometric symbols. Kanzi's mother, with rigorous training, only managed to learn a few symbols, but Kanzi—as a result of exceptional intelligence, early age, or both—had no trouble acquiring many. He initially tried to convey meaning without any regard to word order, but later learned subject-verb-object order. Other captive animals can be trained to be sensitive to grammatical distinctions, including dolphins[23] and European starlings.[24]

We know rather less about the use of complex signals naturally occurring in the wild. There are intriguing anecdotes, and a few careful studies. Both Campbell's monkeys and Diana monkeys—who often forage together—have predator specific alarm calls for leopards and eagles. The two species have distinct alarm calls. Diana monkeys respond to the alarm calls of male Campbell's by giving their own alarm call for the same predator. However, where the predator is more distant, and not an immediate danger, the male Campbell's monkeys preface their alarm with two low "boom" calls. Alarms calls so modified do not elicit corresponding alarm calls by Diana monkeys. This observation was confirmed in carefully controlled playback experiments using recorded alarm calls.[25] Here we have a natural example that combines sender, receiver, eavesdropper, and a complex signal.

We find a higher level of syntactic complexity in bird calls. The black-capped chickadee has a rich system of signals. In particular, the "chickadee" call from which it takes its name has been known for some time to obey rigid syntactic rules. Contrary to the name, there are four—not three—basic acoustic syllables which

[22] Savage-Rumbaugh et al. 1986, and Savage-Rumbaugh and Lewin 1994.
[23] Herman et al. 1984.
[24] Gentner et al. 2006.
[25] Zuberbühler 2002.

are involved in "chickadee," which may be denoted as A, B, C, and D. Playback experiments show that syntactically ill-formed calls are ignored, while well-formed calls evoke a reaction.[26] The rules are (1) any of the basic elements, A, B, C, D may be repeated or omitted, but (2) those that occur must be in the order A, B, C, D. Thus "BCCD" and "ABBCCCD" are well formed, but "ACBBD" and "DCDC" are not.

Two properties of this simple syntax are noteworthy. Given any string whose constituents are only A, B, C, D, it is effectively decidable whether the string is grammatically well formed; you could program a computer to give you the answer. And the class of potential strings that are grammatically well formed is infinite. These properties have sometimes been held up as features unique to human syntax.[27] Chickadee syntax shows us that they are not really so remarkable.

The various chickadee calls appear to convey all kinds of information about group and individual identity, food and predators, but experimental analysis has been slow in coming. In a review article in 1990, Snowdon could comment: "The main limit of this complex grammatical system is that there is no evidence that any of the 362 sequences documented has any functional significance." But more recently it has been shown that information about predator type is encoded in the number of repetitions of D notes in the chickadee call.

Chickadees forage in the brush in small groups. Members of the group often cannot see each other and use calls to keep in contact. They are preyed upon by a large number of different raptors and by a few terrestrial predators, including the domestic cat.

Large raptors, such as the great horned owl, are easier for the small, agile chickadee to evade than small raptors. Raptors in flight can attack rapidly by diving, to which spotted chickadees give a

---

[26] Hailman et al. 1985.
[27] Chomsky 1957 and thereafter. The claim is repeated in Hauser et al. 2002. But compare Pinker and Jackendoff 2005.

special "seet" call. Perched raptors and cats evoke a different response. Chickadees give a version of the chickadee call that functions as a recruitment alarm. On hearing the call, birds do not take cover, but rather mob the predator and drive it away. Presentation experiments with 15 species of live predators showed that the number of D's per call correlates negatively with the size of the predator.[28] There is, no doubt, more to be learned about information content of the full spectrum of chickadee calls.

Alarm calls are about the here and now—or the almost here and now. Honeybees, however, communicate information about how to find distant food sources. That they do so was already known by Aristotle, but he did not know how. Karl von Frisch[29] received a Nobel Prize in 1973 for his analysis of how this information is transmitted through the "waggle dance."

On returning from a new food source close to the hive, a working bee performs a circle dance that motivates others to simply go out and search for the flowers. But if the source is far away, the worker performs a "waggle dance" on a vertical surface. There is a relatively straight run with a zigzag or "waggling" component, followed by circling back and repetition. Bees use the information in the dance to reliably find the vicinity of food sources, and they use scent to home in on them. Although some have found this conclusion hard to accept, is seems now to be well established.[30]

Von Frisch found that the length of the waggling run encodes the distance to the food source and that the angle from the vertical to the main axis of the dance corresponds to the angle from the sun to the food source. To judge this angle accurately the bees must be able to perceive polarization of sunlight, which indeed they can. In fact, it was the analysis of the waggle dance that led to the discovery that bees had this ability to detect polarization.

[28] Tempelton et al. 2005.

[29] von Frisch 1967.

[30] See, for instance, Gould 1975; Riley et al. 2005.

Here we find—for the first time in the chapter—examples of *natural salience*. Correlation of the run with distance needs no explanation. Equating the angle from the vertical to angle from the sun is more of a stretch. But ancestral bees may have danced on an exposed horizontal surface of the hive with the direction of the run pointing directly towards the food source, as is the case in some dwarf honeybees.[31] Subsequent evolution could then have gradually modified the system to its present, more mysterious state— where dancing is vertical, inside the hive, and requires the bees' abilities to detect polarization of light to decode the information.

Honeybees have to cooperate to make their living, and cooperation requires the exchange of information. The waggle dance is only one instance of several signaling systems used by bees.[32] Even simpler organisms have evolved ways of exchanging information to coordinate behavior.

Myxococcus xanthus is social bacterium whose groups have been compared to microbial wolf packs. They forage in the soil, and when they detect groups of other bacteria they exude enzymes that digest them, and they absorb the resulting nutrients.[33] When nutrients are exhausted, and they begin to starve, they aggregate by gliding on slime trails, and differentiate to form a fruiting body. In the interior of the fruiting body some cells differentiate to become spores. These lie dormant until favorable environmental conditions allow the life cycle to repeat. A social group becomes, temporarily, a multicellular organism.[34] All this is accomplished through chemical signals.

Some of these signals are now understood.[35] The first stage of aggregation is triggered by a small molecule produced by starving

---

[31] Dyer and Seeley 1991.

[32] Maynard-Smith and Harper 2003: 115 compare the known vocabularies of honeybees and Vervet monkeys and find that that of the bees is larger.

[33] Berleman, Scott, Chumley, and Kirby 2008.

[34] These prokaryotes have discovered the same survival strategy that is well known in the eukaryotes—the cellular slime molds.

[35] Kaiser 2004.

bacteria, which diffuses through the cell membrane. Low concentrations of this molecule—call it signal A—have no effect, but at a certain threshold concentration, aggregation is initiated. Later, in the process of fruiting body formation, a different signal plays an essential role. This second signal operates locally. It requires end-to-end contact between individual bacteria.

The fact that the concentration of signal A requires a certain threshold to be effective has important consequences for survival. Fruiting body development kills most of the bacteria involved—most don't become spores. The situation must be dire enough to justify this strategy, and there must be enough starving bacteria to carry it out successfully.

This signaling system is an instance of what is called *quorum-sensing*. The name refers to the fact that a quorum must be present for a particular collective action to be carried out successfully. Quorum-sensing was first discovered in 1977 in a bioluminescent marine bacterium (*Vibrio fisheri*) that lives in the light organs of a squid. The bacterium uses quorum-sensing to activate the genes for bioluminescence. The squid turns the light off or on (for the purpose of camouflage) by controlling the concentration of the signal molecule. The squid increases the concentration by providing nutrients to the bacteria, which multiply rapidly. It decreases the concentration by expelling bacteria into the ocean and taking in seawater. On a sunny day, the squid is visible to predators below it as a shadow. It can disguise itself by activating bioluminescence. At night, it is best to turn off the lights.

Since 1977, it has been discovered that quorum-sensing signaling systems are common among bacteria.[36] Some bacteria have multiple quorum-sensing systems, one specific to the species, but others that enable monitoring the concentrations of other species. Within the family of gram-negative bacteria, different species have small modifications of the basic (AHL) signaling molecule, and put it to different uses: to control biofilm formation (like the plaque on your

---

[36] Taga and Bassler 2003; Schauder and Bassler 2001.

teeth), virulence, and spore formation. A different basic signaling circuit is used in gram-positive bacteria to trigger an equally diverse set of behaviors. A third circuit is an interspecies signaling system, shared by both groups. It is sometimes used in infections—for instance in the lungs of those with cystic fibrosis—to help trigger the formation of a mixed species biofilm. Some plants and algae produce molecules that block the quorum-sensing signals used by bacterial infections.[37]

At this level, natural salience almost seems like an understatement. Isn't everything here just chemistry? How could there be any element of conventionality? Well, let's remember that *we* are composed of entities governed by physics and chemistry. Conventionality enters when there is enough plasticity in the signaling interactions to allow alternative signaling systems. For bacteria, biochemistry sets strict rules. But if we look at quorum-sensing over evolutionary time, and reflect on the variety of uses to which the same basic system has been put, we can recover a sense of the plasticity of signaling. Pure convention is gone, but development of the same ancestral signaling system could go one way or another— and in different species of bacteria has done so. Rather than focusing exclusively on pure conventionality, we should also bear in mind cases where there are degrees of conventionality associated with degrees of plasticity in signaling.

Discussions of primate signaling have been dominated by issues imported from human philosophy of mind. What is in the sender's consciousness when she sends the signal and in the hearer's when she receives it? Does the sender have a theory of the receiver's mind, that she uses to predict how the hearer will interpret a signal and respond to it? These are important questions, worthy of careful discussion.

But philosophy of mind will not help us very much in understanding communication in bacteria (or bees, or chickadees), which nevertheless appear to do it quite successfully. The place to start is not with a self-conscious mental theory of meaning, intention, or common knowledge, but rather to focus on *information*. Signals transmit information, and it is the flow of information that makes all life possible.

3

Information

"In the beginning was information. The word came later."

Fred Dretske, *Knowledge and the Flow of Information* (1981)

Epistemology

Dretske was calling for a reorientation in epistemology. He did not think that epistemologists should spend their time on little puzzles[1] or on rehashing ancient arguments about skepticism. Rather, he held that epistemology would be better served by studying the flow of information. Although we may differ on some specifics, I am in fundamental agreement with Dretske.

Information is carried by signals. It flows through signaling networks that not only transmit it, but also filter, combine, and process it in various ways. We can investigate the flow of information using a framework of generalized signaling games. The dynamics of evolution and learning in these games illuminate the creation and flow of information.

---

[1] I must admit to having done some of this, before I knew better.

Information

What is the information in a signal? There are really two questions: *What is the informational content of a signal?* and *What is the quantity of information in a signal?*

Some philosophers have looked at information theory and have seen only an answer to the question of quantity. They do not see an answer to the question of content—or, to use a dangerous word, *meaning*—of a signal. As a result they move to a semantic notion of information, where the informational content in a signal is conceived as a proposition. The information in a signal is to be expressible as "the proposition that____." Signals then, in and out of equilibrium, are thought of as the sorts of things that are either true or false. Dretske takes that road and, as he himself says, it reduces the role of information theory to that of a suggestive metaphor. Others have followed his lead.

I believe that we can do better by using a more general concept of informational content. A new definition of informational content will be introduced here. Informational content, so conceived, fits naturally into the mathematical theory of communication and is a generalization of standard philosophical notions of propositional content.

The *informational content* of a signal consists in how the signal affects probabilities. The *quantity of information* in a signal is measured by how far it moves probabilities. It is easy to see the difference. Suppose, for instance, that there are two states, initially equiprobable. Suppose that signal A moves the probabilities to 9/10 for state 1 and 1/10 for state 2, and that signal B moves the probabilities in exactly the opposite way: 1/10 for state 1 and 9/10 for state 2. Even without knowing exactly how we are going to measure quantity of information, we know by considerations of symmetry that these two signals contain the same amount of information. They move the initial probabilities by the same amount. But they do not have the same *informational content*, because they move the initial probabilities in different directions.

Signal A moves the probability of state 1 up; signal B moves it down.

The key to information is moving probabilities. What probabilities? We use the framework of a sender-receiver signaling game with evolving strategies.[2] That means that we are interested in information not only in equilibrium, but also before interactions have reached equilibrium. It is part of the structure of the game that the states occur with certain probabilities. The probabilities of sender and receiver strategies change over time. In learning dynamics, these probabilities are modified by the learning rule; in evolution they are interpreted as population frequencies changing by differential reproduction. At any given time, in or out of equilibrium, all these probabilities are well defined. Taken together, they give us all the probabilities that we need to assess the content and the quantity of information in a signal at that time.[3] Informational content evolves as strategies evolve.

How should we measure the *quantity of information* in a signal? The information in the signal about a state depends on a comparison of the probability of the state given that this signal was sent and the unconditional probability of the state. We might as well look at the ratio:

$$\mathrm{pr}_{\mathrm{sig}}(\mathrm{state})/\mathrm{pr}(\mathrm{state})$$

where $\mathrm{pr}_{\mathrm{sig}}$ is the probability conditional on getting the signal. This is a key quantity.[4] The way that the signal moves the probability of the state is just by multiplication by this quantity.

But when a signal does not move the probability of a state at all—for instance if the sender sends the same signal in all states—the ratio

---

[2] As always, there is the question of whether the framework is being correctly applied to model the situation of interest. We assume here that it is.

[3] The probabilities never really hit zero or one, although they may converge towards them. So conditional probabilities are well defined. We don't have to worry about dividing by zero. If it appears in an example that we are dividing by zero, throw in a little epsilon.

[4] By Bayes' theorem, the same quantity can be expressed as:

$$\mathrm{pr}(\text{signal given state})/\mathrm{pr}(\text{signal}).$$

is equal to one, but we would like to say that the quantity of information is zero. We can achieve this by taking the logarithm to define the quantity of information as:

$$\log\left[\text{pr}_{\text{sig}}(\text{state})/\text{pr}(\text{state})\right]$$

This is the information in the signal in favor of that state. If we take the logarithm to the base 2, we are measuring the information in *bits*.

A signal carries information about many states, so to get an overall measure of information in the signal we can take a weighted average, with the weights being the probabilities of the states conditional on getting the signal:

$$I_{\text{states}}(\text{signal}) = \sum_i \text{pr}_{\text{sig}}(\text{state i})\log[\text{pr}_{\text{sig}}(\text{state i})/\text{pr}(\text{state i})]$$

This is the average information about states in the signal. It is sometimes called the Kullback–Leibler distance,[5] or the information gained. All this was worked out over 50 years ago,[6] shortly after Claude Shannon published his original paper on information theory. It goes under a slightly different name, *the information provided by an experiment*, in a famous article by Dennis Lindley.[7] Receiving a signal is like looking at the result of an experiment. Alan Turing used almost the same concept in his work breaking the German Enigma code during World War II.[8]

For example, consider our simplest signaling game from Chapter 1, where there are two states, two signals and two acts, with the states equiprobable. A signal moves the probabilities of the states, and how it moves the probability of the second state is determined by how much it moves the probability of the first, so we can plot the average information in the signal as a function of the probability of the first state given the signal. This is shown in figure 3.1:

[5] Although not technically a metric because it is not symmetric.
[6] Kullback and Leibler 1951, and Kullback 1959.
[7] Lindley 1956.
[8] See I. J. Good's preface to *Good Thinking* 1983.

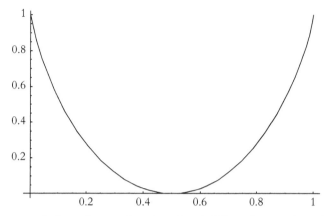

Figure 3.1: Information as a function of probability of state 1 given signal, state initially equiprobable.

If the signal does not move the probability off one-half, the information is 0; if it moves the probability a little, there is a little information; if it moves the probability all the way to one or to zero, the information in the signal is one bit. In a signaling-system equilibrium, one signal moves the probability to one and the other moves it to zero, so each of the two signals carries one bit of information.

The situation is different if the states are not initially equiprobable. Suppose that the probability of state 1 is 6/10 and that of state 2 is 4/10. Then a signal that was sent only in state two would carry more information than one that only came in state one because it would move the initial probabilities more, as shown in figure 3.2:

In a game with four equiprobable states a signal that gives one of the states probability one carries two bits of information about the state. Compare a somewhat more interesting case from Chapter 1, where nature chooses one of four states by independently flipping two fair coins. Coin 1 determines up or down—let us say—and coin 2 determines left or right. The four states, up-left and so on, are equiprobable. There are now two senders. Sender 1 can observe only whether nature has chosen up or down; sender 2 observes whether it is left or right. Each sends one of two signals to the receiver.

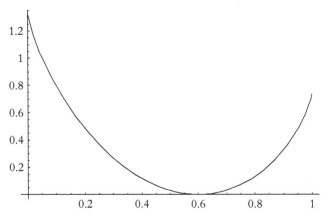

Figure 3.2: Information as a function of probability of state 1 given signal, state 1 initially at probability of .6.

The receiver chooses among four acts, one right for each state.

In an optimal signaling system equilibrium for this little signaling network, pairs of sender signals identify each of the four states with probability one—and the receiver makes the most of the information in the signals. In such a signaling system each signal carries one bit of information. One bit from each of the senders adds up to the two bits we had with one sender and four signals. This is a mathematical convenience of having taken the logarithms to the base 2.

Information about the act

All of the information discussed so far is defined by the probabilities with which nature chooses acts and the probabilities of the sender strategies. But there is also a different kind of information in the signals. We have been discussing *information about the state of nature*, but there is also *information about the act* that will be chosen. The definitions are entirely analogous to those of information about the state.

Taken together, probabilities of the states, probabilities of sender's strategies, and probabilities of receiver's strategies give us unconditional probabilities of the acts. Just add up the probabilities of all combinations that give the act in question its initial probability. Probabilities of receiver's strategies alone give us probabilities of acts given a certain signal. The information in the signal is now measured by how much the signal moves the probabilities of the acts. The average information about the act in a signal is:

$$I_{acts}(\text{signal}) = \sum_i pr_{sig}(\text{act i})\log[pr_{sig}(\text{act i})/pr(\text{act i})]$$

The definition has just the same form and rationale as the definition of information about the state. There are thus two kinds of information in a signal, and two quantities summarizing amounts of information in a signal.

The two quantities need not be the same. For instance, suppose that the sender chooses a different signal for each state but the receiver isn't paying attention and always does the same act. Then there is plenty of information about the states in the signals, but zero information about the acts. Conversely, suppose that the sender chooses signals at random but the receiver uses the signals to discriminate between acts. Then there is zero information about the states in the signals, but there is information about the acts. There may be more states than acts or more acts than states. It is only in special cases where the two quantities of information are the same.

Creation of information in a signal

Let us reflect on what was shown in Chapter 1. Evolution can *create* information. It is not simply a question of learning to use information that is lying around, as is the case when we observe a fixed nature. With natural signs—smoke means fire—the information *about states* is just there, and we need to learn how to utilize it. Nature is *not* playing a game and does not have alternative

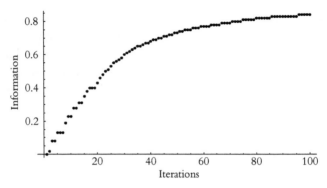

Figure 3.3: Creation of information *ex nihilo* by reinforcement learning.

strategies. Information *about acts* arrives on the scene when we learn to react appropriately to the information about states contained in the smoke. But in signaling games, there may be no initial information about acts or states in the signals. Senders and receivers may just be acting randomly. When evolution (or learning) leads to a signaling system, information is created. Symmetry-breaking shows how information can be created *out of nothing*. Figure 3.3 shows the creation of information about states by reinforcement learning in a two-state, two-signal, two-act signaling game.

Informational content

Now that we know how to measure the quantity of information in a signal, let us return to *informational content*. This is sometimes supposed to be very problematic, but I think that it is remarkably straightforward. Quantity of information is just a summary number—one bit, two bits, etc. *Informational content must be a vector.*[9]

---

[9] This is information content within a given signaling game. It is implicit that this vector applies to the states or acts of *this game*. For a different game, the content vector shows how the signal moves probabilities of different states, or different acts. Content depends on the context of the signaling interaction. It is a modeling decision as to which game is best used to analyze a real situation.

Consider the information in a signal about states, where there are four states. The informational content of a signal tells us how the signal affects the probabilities of each of the four states. It is a vector with four components, one for each state. Each component tells us how the probability of that state moves. So we can take the *informational content* of a signal to be the vector:

$$< \log[\text{pr}_{\text{sig}}(\text{state 1})/\text{pr}(\text{state 1})], \log[\text{pr}_{\text{sig}}(\text{state 2})/\text{pr}(\text{state 2})], ... >$$

The *informational content about acts* in the signal is another vector of the same form.

Suppose that there are four states, initially equiprobable, and signal 2 is sent only in state 2. Then the informational content about states of signal 2 is:

$$I_{\text{States}}(\text{Signal 2}) =< -\infty, 2, -\infty, -\infty >$$

The $-\infty$ components tell you that those states end up with probability zero. (The $-\infty$ is just due to taking the logarithm—no cause for alarm.) The entry for state 2 tells you how much its probability has moved. If the starting probabilities had been different, this entry could have been different. For instance, if the initial probability of this state had been 1/16 with everything else the same, the information about states in signal 2 would have been:

$$I_{\text{States}}(\text{Signal 2}) =< -\infty, 4, -\infty, -\infty >$$

"*Wait a minute,*" someone is sure to say at this point. "*Something very important has been left out!*" What is it? "*But shouldn't the content—at least the declarative content—of a signal be a proposition? And isn't a proposition a set of possible worlds or situations?*"

Suppose a proposition is taken to be a set of states. (States can be individuated finely, and there can be lots of states if you please.) It asserts that the true state is a member of that set. A proposition can just as well be specified by giving the set of states that the true state is not in. That is what the $-\infty$ components of the information vector do. If a signal carries propositional information, that information can be read off the informational content vector. For instance, if the signal "tells you" that it is "state 2 or state 4" in our example, then the content vector will have the form:

$$I_{States}(Signal\ 2) = < -\infty, \underline{\quad}, -\infty, \underline{\quad} >$$

with the minus infinity components ruling out states 1 and 3, and the blanks being filled by numbers specifying how the probabilities of state 2 and 4 have moved.

That is to say that the familiar notion of propositional content as a set of possible situations is a rather special case of the much richer information-theoretic account of content. This vector specifies more than the propositional content. Furthermore, some signals will not have propositional content at all. This will be typical in out-of-equilibrium states of the signaling game. It is the traditional account that has left something out.

Notice that the *quantity* of information in a signal—as measured by Kullback and Leibler—is just gotten by averaging over the components of the informational content vector. It is a kind of summary obtained from informational content.

If we average again we get the average quantity of information in the signals. This quantity is called *mutual information*. If we take the maximum of this over signaling system equilibria, we get a measure of the information transfer capacity in the signaling game. There is a seamless integration of this conception of content with classical information theory.

Intentionality and teleosemantics

Some philosophers take the view that real information presupposes *intentionality* and that consequently the mathematical theory of information is irrelevant to informational content. The semantic notion of information is conflated with the question of intentionality. What is intentionality? It is a said to be a kind of directedness towards an object. That doesn't tell us much, and doesn't explain why anyone should think it was not part of mathematical information theory. Signals, after all, do carry information directed toward the states and information directed toward the acts.

The philosophical history of the concept of intentionality tells us more. It starts with Franz Brentano,[10] who held that intentionality was what distinguished the mental from the physical. If what is being left out is a model of the mental life of the agents, then I would say that it should be left out when the agents lack a mental life and put in when they do. I would not speculate on the mental life of bees; to talk of the mental life of bacteria seems absurd; and yet signaling plays a vital biological role in both cases. Some may want to define signals so that these are not "real" signals, but I fail to see the point of such maneuvers. Rather, I would treat the case where agents have a mental life as a special case. If we have a reasonable model of the relevant aspects of mental life, we can put them in the model. We move some way in this direction in the next section, where we consider subjective information.

Some have swallowed the requirement of intentionality or something quite like it, but have tried to let Mother Nature (in the form of evolution) supply the intentionality. As John Maynard Smith puts it: "In biology, the use of informational terms implies intentionality, in that both the form of the signal, and the response to it, have evolved by selection. Where an engineer sees design, a biologist sees natural selection."[11] This is roughly the idea behind Ruth Millikan's *teleosemantics*. An evolved signal has a directedness, or intentionality, in virtue of the Darwinian fitness accrued by its use.[12]

I say about teleosemantic intentionality the same thing I said about mentalistic intentionality. If we have a good model where it applies, it can be added to the theory. But neither intentionality nor

[10] Brentano 1874.

[11] Maynard Smith 2000.

[12] See Millikan 1984. For other teleosemantic theories that do not share Millikan's basic commitment to a picture theory of meaning see Papineau 1984, 1987.

teleosemantics is required to give an adequate account of the informational content of signals. Here I stand with Dretske. The information is just *there*. At this point some philosophers will say "You might as well say that Smoke carries information about fire." Well, doesn't it? Don't fossils carry information about past life forms? Doesn't the cosmic background radiation carry information about the early stages of the universe? *The world is full of information.* It is not the sole province of biological systems. What is special about biology is that the form of information transfer is driven by adaptive dynamics.

Objective and subjective information

None of the probabilities used so far are degrees of belief of sender and receiver. They are objective probabilities, determined by nature and the evolutionary or learning process. Organisms (or organs) playing the role of sender and receiver need have no cognitive capacities.

But suppose that they do. Suppose that a sender and receiver are human and that they try to think rationally about the signaling game. Suppose that the sender has subjective probabilities over the receiver's strategies and the receiver has subjective probabilities over the sender's strategies, and that both have subjective probabilities over the states. These subjective probabilities are just degrees of belief; they may not be in line with the objective probabilities at all. Then each signal carries *two additional kinds of subjective information*. There is *subjective information about how the receiver will react*, which lives in the sender's degrees of belief. This is of interest to a sender who wants to get a receiver to do something. There is *subjective information about what state the sender observed*, which lives in the receiver's degrees of belief. This is of interest to a receiver who wants to use the sender as a source of information about the states. Both sender and receiver use these kinds of information in decision making. Both sender and receiver strive (1) to act optimally given their subjective probabilities, and (2) to learn to bring subjective probabilities in concordance with the objective probabilities in the world. They may or may not succeed. When we are applying the account to beings that can reasonably be thought to have subjective probabilities, such as perhaps ourselves,[13] we now have at least four types of informational content—two objective and two subjective. If the signaling game is more complex, for instance if there is an eavesdropper, the informational structure becomes richer.

The flow of information

In the signaling equilibrium of a Lewis sender-receiver game, information is transmitted from sender to receiver, but it is only in the most trivial sense that we can be said to have a *flow* of information. As a preview of coming attractions (Chapters 11, 13, 14) and as an example of flow, let us consider a little signaling *chain*.

There are a sender, an intermediary, and a receiver. Nature chooses one of two states with equal probability. The sender observes the state, chooses one of two signals, and sends it to the intermediary; the intermediary observes the sender's signal, chooses one of her own two signals, and sends it to the receiver. (The intermediary's set of signals may or may not match that of the sender.) The receiver observes the intermediary's signal and chooses one of two acts. If the act matches the state, sender, intermediary and receiver all get a payoff of one, otherwise a payoff of zero.

It is tempting to assume that these agents already have signaling for simpler sender-receiver interactions to build upon. But even if they do not, adaptive dynamics can carry them to a signaling system, as shown in figure 3.4:

---

[13] Modern psychology details systematic departures from this idealized picture.

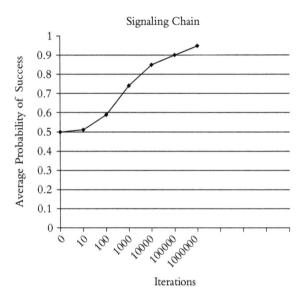

Figure 3.4: Emergence of a signaling chain *ex nihilo* by reinforcement learning.

Although reinforcement learning succeeds in creating a signaling chain without a pre-existing signaling background, notice that it takes a much longer time than in the simpler two-agent model.

The speed with which the chain signaling system can be learned is much improved if the sender and receiver have pre-existing signaling systems. They need not even be the same signaling system. Sender and receiver can have different "languages" so that the intermediary has to act as a "translator", or signal transducer. One could even consider an extreme case in which the sender and receiver used the same tokens as signals but with opposite meanings. "For example, sender's and receiver's strategies are:

SENDER	RECEIVER
State 1 ⇒ red	red ⇒ Act 2
State 2 ⇒ blue	blue ⇒ Act 1

A successful translator must learn to receive one signal and send another, so that the chain leads to a successful outcome.

SENDER	TRANSLATOR	RECEIVER
State 1 ⇒ red	see red ⇒ send blue	blue ⇒ Act 1
State 2 ⇒ blue	see blue ⇒ send red	red ⇒ Act 2

The translator's learning problem is really quite simple, and she can learn to complete the chain very quickly."

In this signaling chain equilibrium, the sender's signal to the translator contains one bit of information about the state and the translator's signal to the receiver contains one bit of information about the state. And on any play, the translator's signal to the receiver has the same *informational content* as the sender's signal to her. Information *flows* from sender through translator to receiver. The receiver then acts *just as she would have if she had observed the state directly*.

That is, of course, the ideal case. Some information can get lost along the way because of noise or error.[14]

Using our notion of the content of a signal, there is no difficulty in allowing for gradual degradation of content. Information can flow through longer signaling chains and through more complex signaling networks. Some informational content may get lost. This may even be beneficial if extraneous information needs to be filtered out. We will see how information from different sources may be integrated in ways that include logical inference and computation of truth values as special cases. Signaling networks of different kinds are the locus of information transmission and processing at all levels of biological and social organization. The study of information processing in signaling networks is a new direction for naturalistic epistemology.

---

[14] Here I part company with Dretske 1981: 57–8.

4

Evolution

"such things survived, being organized spontaneously in a fitting way; whereas those which grew otherwise perished and continue to perish...."

Aristotle, *Physics*[1]

Evolution

The ideas of natural selection and survival of the fittest existed already in Greek philosophy. Aristotle is not describing his own view—he believed in the fixity of the species—but rather a rival theory according to which unsuccessful species go to extinction. Aristotle is referring to Empedocles of Sicily.[2] Empedocles was a statesman and a physician as well as a mystic, philosopher, and poet. His theory was put forward in a long poem, *On Nature*. Empedocles' account of the origin of species begins with a haphazard combination of parts into a great variety of organisms, only the fittest of which survived. Empedocles influenced Democritus, and both Empedocles and Democritus influenced Lucretius. As Lucretius puts it in his own poem, *On the Nature of Things*:

---

[1] Aristotle, *Physics* II 8, 198b29.

[2] There are secondary sources, such as Simplicius' commentary on the foregoing passage in Aristotle's *Physics*, and Lucretius' poem. See Sedley 2003b and Campbell 2003 on the connections between Empedocles and Lucretius.

Perforce there perished many a stock, unable:
By propagation to forge a progeny.

Empedocles even had a theory of how traits are transmitted from generation to generation. Small copies of organs form in the male and female, and in reproduction some from the father and some from the mother combine to form the new organism.

He thus has in hand a rudimentary theory of recombination. Empedocles influenced Hippocrates (probably both directly and through Democritus). Hippocrates' theory of inheritance is remarkably similar to that put forward by Darwin in *The Variation of Plants and Animals under Domestication* nine years after the publication of *The Origin of Species*.[3] Darwin did not know about Hippocrates at the time, but in a letter to William Ogle in 1868, Darwin writes:

I thank you most sincerely for your letter, which is very interesting to me. I wish I had known of these views of Hippocrates before I had published, for they seem almost identical with mine—merely a change of terms— and an application of them to classes of facts necessarily unknown to the old philosopher. The whole case is a good illustration of how rarely anything is new.

Darwin and Hippocrates were wrong about inheritance. But Darwin was right about the broad outlines of the theory of evolution. Traits are inherited by some unknown mechanism. There is some process that produces natural variation in these traits. The traits may affect the ability of the organism to reproduce, and thus the average number of individuals bearing the traits in the next generation. Therefore, those traits that enhance reproductive success increase in frequency in the population, and those that lead to reproductive success below the average

---

[3] I owe my knowledge of Darwin's theory to my colleague P. Kyle Stanford. See Stanford 2007.

decrease in frequency. The three essential factors in Darwin's account are (i) *natural variation*, (ii) *differential reproduction*, and (iii) *inheritance*.

Evolutionarily stable strategies

Darwinian processes lead to adaptation to a fixed environment, at least where the genetic mechanism doesn't get in the way.[4] The story is more complicated when fitness depends on the frequencies of different types who interact with one another. Here the fitness landscape may be constantly changing, along with the population proportions. John Maynard Smith, following the lead of William Hamilton,[5] realized that this kind of interactive evolution is a biological version of von Neumann and Morgenstern's Theory of Games.[6]

In 1973, John Maynard Smith and George Price introduced a strengthening of the Nash equilibrium concept of game theory— the concept of an *evolutionarily stable strategy*. The context was the explanation of "limited war" in animal contests. Since hyper-aggressive types, Hawks, defeat peaceful types, Doves, to win resources, why don't they take over the population? The general answer is that selection here is frequency-dependent. If most of the population is occupied by Hawks, they usually interact with each other in fights that lead to serious injury or death. It is only good to be a Hawk if there are enough Doves around to exploit.

Hawk–Dove interactions are modeled as a game. Payoffs for a typical example are shown in the following table, with the numbers being payoffs (in Darwinian fitness) of row strategy against column strategy:

	Hawk	Dove
Hawk	0	3
Dove	1	2

(In our evolutionary context, payoffs only depend on strategies, not on who is row and who is column. The whole payoff table listing *row payoff, column payoff* in each cell looks like this:

	Hawk	Dove
Hawk	0, 0	3, 1
Dove	1, 3	2, 2

In what follows we will use the first, simpler form of giving evolutionary games.)

It is evident that where you are meeting Hawks, it is better to be a Dove (column 1) and where you are meeting Doves (column 2) it is better to be a Hawk. Consequently, a population of All Hawks cannot be evolutionarily stable in that in such a population a few mutant Doves would do better than the natives. Likewise a population of All Doves would be vulnerable to invasion by a few Hawks.

An evolutionarily stable strategy in one such that if the whole population played it, a few mutants would always do worse against the resulting population (including the mutants) than the natives would. Thus the mutants would fade away. If the population is large and individuals are randomly paired to have an interaction there is a simple test for evolutionary stability in terms of the payoffs to the game. A strategy, S, is evolutionarily stable if for any other strategy, M, either:

(i) Fitness (S played against S) > Fitness (M played against S) or:

(ii) Fitnesses are equal against S, but Fitness(S against M) > Fitness(M against M)

This is how evolutionary stability is defined by Maynard Smith and Price.[7]

For instance, in the Hawk–Dove game Hawk is not evolutionarily stable because Fitness (Hawk against Hawk) is less than Fitness (Dove against Hawk). Dove is not evolutionarily stable because Fitness (Dove against Dove) is less than Fitness (Hawk against Dove).

The Maynard Smith–Price test is easily applied to other familiar simple games. For instance, consider the Stag Hunt game. Players can either hunt *Stag* or hunt *Hare*. Hunting Stag is a cooperative enterprise. It fails if both players do not hunt Stag, but it pays off well if they do. Hare hunting is a solitary enterprise. Hare hunters do equally well if the other hunts Hare or Stag, but worse than successful Stag hunters. The Stag Hunt has this kind of payoff structure:

	Hare	Stag
Hare	3	3
Stag	0	4

Applying the test of Maynard Smith and Price, we see that both *Stag* and *Hare* are evolutionarily stable strategies. Stag against Hare does worse than Hare against Hare; Hare against Stag does worse than Stag against Stag. A population of each type is stable against invasion by a few mutants of the other type.

For an example where there is exactly one evolutionarily stable strategy, consider the most widely discussed game theory model in the social sciences, the Prisoner's Dilemma:

[7] If the first condition is satisfied, mutants are driven out rapidly. If the second condition holds, mutants fade away more slowly.

	Cooperate	Defect
Cooperate	3	1
Defect	4	2

Defect is an evolutionarily stable strategy; cooperate is not.

But what about all the models that explain the evolution of altruism, which is usually taken as cooperation in the Prisoner's Dilemma? All these accounts, in one way or another, explain the evolution of cooperation by some correlation mechanism.[8] Cooperators tend to meet cooperators; defectors tend to meet defectors. Pairing is not random. If pairing is not random the Maynard Smith–Price test of evolutionary stability is *wrong*. This is transparent if correlation is perfect. Then a population of defectors could be invaded by a few mutant cooperators. The cooperators meet each other for a payoff of 3, while the native defectors have a payoff of 2. Correlation can change everything.

Differential reproduction

Stability is really a dynamic concept. A rest state is *strongly stable* if all states near to it are carried to it by the dynamics. You could think of a marble at the bottom of a bowl. It is just *stable* if states near to it are not carried away by the dynamics. Think of the marble sitting on table top as being stable but not strongly stable. Otherwise it is unstable, like a marble balanced at the top of an inverted bowl. Maynard Smith and Price clearly have in mind something like dynamic stability. Where is the dynamics?

To build a dynamic foundation for the notion of an evolution-arily stable strategy, Taylor and Jonker introduced the *replicator dynamics*.[9] This is a model of differential reproduction in a large

---

[8] See Bergstrom 2002; Skyrms 1996, 2004.
[9] Taylor and Jonker 1978.

population, where types are inherited with complete fidelity. For simplicity, Mendelian genetics is left out of the picture. Reproduction proceeds as if by cloning.

Replicator dynamics is driven by *Darwinian fitness*—expected number of progeny. If the expected number of progeny of a type is for instance two, then some individuals might have four and some three and some one or zero. But in a large enough population these differences will almost surely average out, and the average number of progeny will equal the expectation. On average, you get what you expect. This gives us replicator dynamics as introduced by Taylor and Jonker to provide a dynamical foundation for evolutionary game theory.

Suppose that reproduction takes place in discrete time—for instance, every spring. What proportion $x_{new}(S)$ of the new generation will play a given strategy, S? It is just the number who play S in the new population divided by total number in the population. The number who play S in the new population is equal to the total number in the old population, N, multiplied by the proportion who had strategy S, $x_{old}(S)$, multiplied by the average number for offspring of those who had strategy S, Fitness(S). We have to divide this by the total number of the new population which is just the number of the old population, N, multiplied by the average number of offspring throughout the old population, Average Fitness.

$$x_{new} = [N \ x_{old}(S)Fitness(S)]/[N \ Average \ Fitness]$$

N drops out and we get x_{new} from x_{old} by multiplying by a Darwinian success factor:

$$x_{new} = x_{old}[Fitness(S)/Average \ Fitness]$$

This is discrete time replicator dynamics. There is an associated (idealized) continuous time replicator dynamics that gives the rate of change of population proportions, dx/dt at a point in time:

$$dx/dt = x[Fitness(S) — Average \ Fitness]$$

This is what Taylor and Jonker gave us as a simple model of differential reproduction.

What about *cultural evolution*? We want to discuss dynamics of signaling for cultural evolution as well as for biological evolution. There are cases of each, and mixed cases, that are all of interest. We would like a theory of cultural evolution to be more than just a story about how culture evolved. In all honesty, a full theory at this point is out of the question; the cognitive processes involved are too various, complex and poorly understood. The best we can do is to start with a simple basic model that we have some hope of understanding.

One basic process is *imitation*. Suppose that individuals look around them and see which behaviors or strategies are paying off for others, and imitate those strategies with probability proportional to their success. This process and a number of variations on it have been analyzed.[10] What we get, when the population is large and chance fluctuations average out, is just our simple model of differential reproduction—*the replicator dynamics*.[11]

But what is the currency here, in which payoffs are measured? It has to be whatever drives differential imitation. This has to be empirically determined for the context of application. The specific application of the theory derives its content from this determination. The relevant payoffs for cultural evolution may or may not correlate well with Darwinian fitness. In conditions of hardship, both may correlate with eating well and surviving attacks of predators; in conditions of affluence they may be decoupled. Even if the form of the dynamics is the same for biological and cultural evolution the substantive conclusions may be different. Care in interpretation is required.

The replicator dynamics may or may not lead to a dynamical equilibrium (a rest point of the dynamics). If individuals are paired at random and there are just two strategies, it must do so. We can

---

[10] Björnerstedt and Weibull 1995; Weibull 1995; Schlag 1998.
[11] Or some slight variant. This route to the replicator dynamics is even more straightforward, because there is no diploid genetics being suppressed.

visualize the situation by plotting the proportion of one of the strategies on an interval from 0 to 1. We could have:

(i) the dynamics carrying one strategy to fixation, no matter what the interior starting point:

(ii) the dynamics carrying the population to a mixed state, no matter what the starting point:

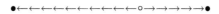

(iii) the dynamics carrying one or the other strategy to fixation, depending on the starting point:

$$\bullet \leftarrow \leftarrow \leftarrow \leftarrow \leftarrow \leftarrow \leftarrow \leftarrow \leftarrow \leftarrow \circ \rightarrow \rightarrow \rightarrow \rightarrow \rightarrow \bullet$$

(iv) the dynamics not moving at all:

. . . .

Case (i) is exemplified by the Prisoner's Dilemma. *All cooperate* is a rest point of the dynamics because defectors are all extinct.[12] But it is dynamically unstable. We mark an unstable rest point with a hollow point. All other points are carried to *All Defect*, which is dynamically strongly stable. We mark a strongly stable rest point with a filled circle. With Hawk-Dove, we have case (ii). *All Hawk* and *All Dove* are dynamically unstable. The dynamically stable equilibrium is a mixed (or polymorphic) state of the population with some Hawks and some Doves. The Stag Hunt is case (iii). Here the polymorphic rest state is an unstable "knife-edge." Any movement off it carries the population to one of the strongly stable equilibria—*All Stag* or *All Hare*.

---

[12] Differential reproduction by itself does not introduce new types.

For case (iv) consider the *game of inconsequential actions*. Here the available actions have no payoff consequences whatever. I believe that much of life has this structure.

	Do This	Do That
Do This	o	o
Do That	o	o

Replicator dynamics does not move any point. (We can't really draw it.) All points are *Stable* in that nearby points stay nearby, but no state is *strongly stable*.

The Red Queen

When we have three strategies, however, replicator dynamics may not lead to equilibrium at all! Consider the familiar game of *rock-scissors-paper*. Rock breaks scissors, scissors cuts paper, paper covers rock, so we get the following sort of payoffs:

| Rock–scissors–paper | | |
	R	S	P
R	I	2	o
S	o	I	2
P	2	o	I

This structure is also found outside children's games. Christof Hauert, Silvia de Monte, Josef Hofbauer, and Karl Sigmund find rock-scissors-paper structure in a social dilemma with the possibility of opting out.[13]

The pure social dilemma is a generalization of the Prisoner's Dilemma to many players. Individuals can either choose to contribute to the public good or to free ride. Contributions are

---

[13] Hauert et al. 2002.

multiplied by the synergy of the joint project, and the joint public good is divided among everyone. If everyone contributes everyone does well. But the multiplier is smaller than the group number, so your dollar contribution gets you personally less than a dollar in return although it can get the group much more. Thus, whatever others do, it is in an agent's own selfish interest to free-ride and share the benefits of others' contributions. If everyone free rides, the public good project fails. There is nothing to distribute, and all do very poorly. Thus we have the n-Person Prisoner's dilemma. To this basic setup is added the possibility of opting out and being a loner. Loners are less successful than those in cooperative groups, but more successful than those in failed public-goods projects. In a population of cooperators, free-riders do better than natives. In a population of free-riders, loners do better. In a population of loners, cooperators do better.

Barry Sinervo and Curtis Lively find rock-scissors-paper structure in mating strategies of side-blotched lizards in California.[14] There are three types of males, which exhibit different coloration. Orange-throated males are very aggressive and guard large territories. Blue-throated males guard smaller territories and are able to guard their mates. Yellow-throated males resemble females, and mate with females on the sly. In a population of mate-guarding blue throats, the ultra-dominant orange throats do better. But they can be invaded by yellow-throated sneakers. And these can be invaded in turn by the blue throats. Field studies confirm the presence of cycles.

Benjamin Kirkup and Margaret Riley find rock-paper-scissors being played by bacteria in the gut of a living mouse.[15] One strain of *E.coli* both produces a poison and maintains immunity to this poison. There are two metabolic costs, one for the poison and one for the immunity, which reduce reproductive potential. These poisoners beat normal *E.coli*, which are not immune, in the

[14] Sinervo and Lively 1996.
[15] Kirkup and Riley 2004.

spatial interactions in the gut. A third strain maintains immunity to the poison, but does not produce it. It free-rides, so to speak, on the spite of the poisoners.

These free-riders flourish in a population of poisoners, because of the lower metabolic load. But in a population of such free-riders, the normals will do best. Here there is no poison, and the cost of maintaining immunity is a drag on the free riders. This rock-scissors–paper type of interaction structure explains the maintenance of all three types in the wild. As the Red Queen said to Alice, "*Now, here, you see, it takes all the running you can do, to keep in the same place.*"

The replicator dynamics for rock-scissors-paper is shown in figure 4.1.

Rock-scissors-paper has four rest points (or equilibria) of the replicator dynamics. The three possible pure populations (*all rock*, *all scissors*, *all paper*) are all dynamically unstable. The other equilibrium is the mixed state where one-third of the population plays each strategy. This is stable, since points near it stay near it, but not strongly stable. The equilibria are not so important here. No initial population state that is not already an equilibrium converges to any of the equilibria.

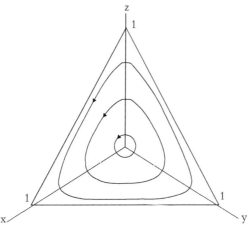

Figure 4.1: Cycles in rock-scissors-paper.

This changes if we modify the payoffs slightly:[16]

Rock-scissors-paper II

For small positive ε, trajectories of the replicator dynamics spiral inward to the point where the population proportions are equal.

	R	S	P
R	1-ε	2	0
S	0	1-ε	2
P	2	0	1-ε

This equilibrium has changed character. It is not only stable; it is *strongly stable*. Population states near it get carried to it. More impressively, it is *globally stable*. Every state in which none of the strategies is extinct converges to it.

The example illustrates another concept that will be important to us. The tiniest change in the dynamics changed the equilibrium structure radically. (A negative ε rather than a positive one would have caused the trajectories to spiral outward, changing the central equilibrium from stable to unstable.) Our original rock-scissors–paper game with replicator dynamics is said to be *structurally unstable*. In a structurally unstable situation, small local changes in the rates of change of population proportions can lead to a radically different global dynamic structure. Our game of inconsequential actions was also structurally unstable. The littlest consequence could change everything. Although structural instability in the replicator dynamics is rare in the space of games in general, in signaling games it happens *all the time*!

[16] Zeeman 1980; Hofbauer and Sigmund 1998.

Natural variation

Let us now add Darwin's third principle—natural variation. In a Mendelian setting, sexual reproduction adds a lot of natural variation through genetic recombination of contributions from both parents—just as Empedocles shrewdly hypothesized. But in line with our minimalist approach so far, preserving compatibility with both biological and cultural evolution, we will just add *mutation*.

With high probability types or strategies are inherited, but with some small probability any type may mutate into any other. On the cultural side these mutations may be viewed as imperfect imitation, leavened by error, which keeps all strategies in play and prevents an absolutely monomorphic culture. In principle it might be easier for a given type to mutate into a second than into a third. However, we will concentrate on the case of uniform mutation. Every type has the same probability of mutating into any other type, so there is only one mutation rate. We again assume a large population, so chance fluctuations average out. This gives us *replicator-mutator* dynamics.[17]

Those population states that were dynamic equilibria only by virtue of all other types being extinct do not survive mutation. Consider one population playing Prisoner's Dilemma:

	Cooperate	Defect
Cooperate	3	1
Defect	4	2

With replicator dynamics there are two equilibria, *All Cooperate* and *All Defect*. The former is unstable, since introduction of any defectors would lead to them taking over the population. With replicator-mutator dynamics, defectors are automatically introduced by mutation and only one equilibrium survives. This is the *All Defect*

---

[17] Introduced by Hadeler 1981 and analyzed by Hofbauer 1985.

equilibrium perturbed slightly by mutation. For a small mutation rate it is an *Almost-All Defect* equilibrium.

Let us return to our original rock-scissors-paper game. Instead of changing the payoffs a little, as we did earlier, we can keep the payoffs the same but introduce mutation. We change the dynamics to replicator-mutator with a small mutation rate. Since we are starting with a structurally unstable situation, we expect that this small change might have large consequences. Indeed, it is so. As before, all cycles vanish and the only surviving equilibrium is the population state where each of rock, scissors, and paper is played with probability 1/3. This is a global attractor—all trajectories lead to it. Since mutants from more frequent strategies to less frequent ones are more numerous than those in the converse direction, mutation gives the dynamics a little nudge in the direction of equality. That is all it takes to destabilize the cycles and turn them into inward spirals.

Rock-scissors-paper has a lot to teach us about evolutionary games. The first big lesson is the importance of dynamical analysis. If we look for evolutionarily stable strategies—strategies that if established could repel any invaders—there aren't any. If we concentrate on equilibrium analysis, we miss the cycles. The second big lesson is the importance of attention to structural stability. If the model is structurally unstable, a small change in the model may make a big change in its dynamics.

5

Evolution in Lewis Signaling Games

"The emergence of meaning is a moral certainty"

    Brian Skyrms, *Evolution of the Social Contract*

"Something is morally certain if its probability comes so close to complete certainty that the difference cannot be perceived."

    Jacob Bernoulli, *The Art of Conjecture*

That was the bold claim I made in 1996 about the evolution of signaling systems. Signaling systems had been shown to be the only evolutionarily stable strategies in n–state, n–signal, (and here) n–act signaling games. They were the only attractors in the replicator dynamics. In simple cases, like those discussed in Chapter 1, it was clear why almost every possible starting point was carried to a signaling system. How far do these positive results generalize?

The good news

Consider the two–state, two–signal, two–act, signaling game where nature chooses the states with equal probability. In Chapter 1, we restricted the strategies to those that might be used by those who have signaling in mind. The sender sent a different signal in each state. The receiver picked a different act for each signal. They knew at the onset that states and signals were important, they just hadn't settled on a signaling system. This is making things too easy. Let's put in all possible strategies.

Senders now have two additional strategies: Always send signal 1, always send signal 2. Receivers also have two additional strategies: Always do act 1, always do act 2.

The sender's strategies ignore the state and the receiver's strategies ignore the signal. Why not? We may have a population of senders and a population of receivers. In this case there are four possible strategies represented in each population. Alternatively, there may be a single population where an individual is sometimes in the role of sender and sometimes in the role of receiver. A strategy for an individual specifies what to do when in the role of sender and what to do in the role of receiver. There are 16 possible strategies. What happens?

Everything still works fine. Signaling always evolves, both in one-population and two-population contexts. We can't draw pictures with all the strategies included, but it is still possible to establish that almost every initial point is carried to a signaling system.[1] It can be shown that average payoff increases along every trajectory of the dynamics. Then there can't be cycles like those in rock-scissors-paper. Evolutionary dynamics has to go to an equilibrium. But there are lots of new equilibria when we include all strategies. Notably, there are *pooling equilibria*, in which the sender ignores the state and the receiver ignores the signal. However, it can be shown that all the equilibria other than signaling systems are dynamically unstable. Evolution won't hit them. There are no pictures, but the story is just like that in Chapter 1.

Bad news: states with unequal probabilities

The foregoing is in the context where nature chooses states with equal probability. That is the simplest case, but there is no reason

---

[1] Huttegger 2007a; Hofbauer and Huttegger 2008.

why nature may not choose states with unequal probability: 60%–40%, 90%–10%, or 99%–1%. Then the pooling equilibria take the form where senders transmit no information and receivers ignore the signal and always do the act suited to the most likely state.

If the more likely state is *very* likely, players in such an equilibrium may do quite well. We can no longer make the case that the mutant signalers will do as well against the natives as the natives do against each other. If both signals are sent at random (but ignored by receivers) in the native population, then mutants pursuing a signaling system strategy will be led to do the wrong act half the time, when they receive a native's signal. They will do perfectly against each other, but most of their interactions are with natives. So they make lots of mistakes, while the natives usually do the right thing. They will do worse than the natives.

For a two-population setting, consider a case where state 1 occurs 90% of the time and state 2 10%. Then a receiver who *always does act 1*, no matter what the signal, gains average payoff of .9. He does the right act for the state 90% of the time and misses 10% of the time. So he does reasonably well without any information transmission. Consider such a population of receivers paired with a polymorphic population of senders, half of whom always send signal 1 and half of whom always send signal 2. Everyone gets an average payoff of .9. Introduce a few senders who discriminate states, and they will do no better and no worse than the natives. But if we introduce a few receivers who discriminate between signals to coordinate with the few senders, they will do very badly against the natives. Against the natives they will get an average payoff of only .5. That was good enough to get a foot in the door when the states were equiprobable and the natives were making .5, but it is not good enough when the states are not equiprobable. Now evolutionary dynamics will sometimes hit signaling systems and sometimes hit pooling equilibria, with the likelihood of the latter increasing with the disparity in probability between the states. The bottom line in both the one- and two-population cases is that *evolution of signaling is no longer guaranteed*. How serious is this problem?

Evolution can lead to pooling equilibria *where no information is transmitted* whenever states have unequal probability. It can also lead to signaling systems. It is more likely that we get pooling the larger the disparity in probabilities of the states, but the impact on the welfare of the players is smaller.

Some good news

Our pooling equilibria, where no information is transferred are characterized by (i) the receivers ignoring the signal and always doing the right thing for the most probable state and senders ignoring the state, either by (a) always sending signal 1 or (b) always sending signal 2. Any mix of senders of types (a) and (b) gives us a pooling equilibrium. Thus there is a *line* of such equilibria, corresponding to the proportion of the two types of sender. The endpoints, representing all one type of sender or all the other type, are unstable. Each endpoint can be destabilized by a few signaling system mutants, of an appropriate kind. But evolution can lead to any of the other points corresponding to a mixed population of different types of senders.

A line of equilibria is *structurally unstable*, like the concentric orbits in the rock-scissors-paper example of the last chapter. A small change in the dynamics can make a big change in the set of equilibria. So far the dynamics have been pure differential reproduction. We can modify the dynamics a little bit by putting in a little natural variation in the form of mutation.

The analysis for two populations has been carried out by Josef Hofbauer and Simon Huttegger. The replicator dynamics is replaced with its natural generalization, the *replicator-mutator* dynamics.[2] Each generation reproduces according to replicator dynamics but $(1-\varepsilon)$ of the progeny of each type breed true and ε of the progeny mutate to all types with equal probability. (Self-mutation

[2]   Hadeler 1981; Hofbauer 1985.

is allowed.) Taking the continuous time limit gives the replicator-mutator dynamics.

A little uniform mutation (no matter how little) collapses the line of pooling equilibria to a single point. (This is intuitively reasonable. If the receivers are disregarding the signals, there is no selection pressure on the senders. If one type of sender, (a) or (b), is more numerous, more mutate out than mutate in.) The big question concerns the character of this one point. *Is it an attractor* that pulls nearby states to it? *Is it dynamically unstable*, so that for all practical purposes we needn't worry about it?

It depends. For states whose probabilities are not too unequal, this pooling point is unstable. Then our original positive result is restored. Signaling always evolves! That's the good news. But for when one state is much more probable than the other, the pooling point is an attractor. Signaling sometimes evolves, sometimes not. That's the not so good news. For equal and small mutation rates for both senders and receivers, Hofbauer and Huttegger calculate the probability where the switch takes place.[3] It is between .78 and .79.

That's not too bad. Up to probability 3/4, a little mutation assures that almost all initial points evolve to signaling systems. Things are even more favorable, if the receivers have a higher mutation rate than the senders. If receivers experiment twice as often as senders, paradise is regained. The bad equilibrium with no information transfer is always dynamically unstable, for any (positive) state probabilities. But we cannot assume that such favorable mutation rates are always in place.

In addition, we should notice that these are results for payoffs that are all 0 for failures and all 1 for successes. For very infrequent states where the payoffs are much more important—such as the presence of a predator—the disparity in payoffs can balance the disparity in probabilities. Predators may be rare, but it does not pay to disregard them.

This consideration can restore almost sure evolution of signaling for rare events.

---

[3] Technically, this is called a "bifurcation."

More bad news: partial pooling

What happens when we move to three states, three signals, and three acts? We go back to the favorable assumption that all states are chosen with equal probability. Nevertheless, a whole new class of equilibria appears. Suppose that a sender sends signal 1 in both states 1 and 2, and in state 3 sends either signal 2 or 3 with probabilities x and (1−x) respectively. And suppose that the receiver, on getting signals 2 or 3 always does act 3, but on getting signal 1 does either act 1 or act 2 with probabilities y and (1−y) respectively. This is shown in figure 5.1

For any combination of values of x and y as population proportions, including 0 and 1, we have a population state that is a dynamic equilibrium. We thus have an infinite set of equilibrium components. Considering x going from 0 to 1 and y going from 0 to 1, we can visualize this set as a square of equilibria. These equilibria pool states 1 and 2 together, but do not pool all states together—so they are called *partial pooling* equilibria.[4] Because information is imperfectly transmitted, sender and receiver succeed 2/3 of the time. In comparison, total pooling would give a payoff of only 1/3, and perfect signaling would give a payoff of 1.

3 by 3 by 3

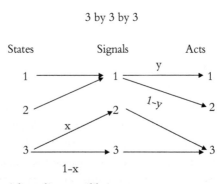

Figure 5.1: Partial pooling equilibria.

[4] There is likewise a square of partial pooling equilibria that lumps states 2 and 3 together, and one that pools states 1 and 3.

In total pooling equilibria, where all states are lumped together, no information is transmitted. In partial pooling equilibria, some information is transmitted, but not as much as would be in a signaling system.

If we run simulations of evolutionary dynamics in 3 state, 3 signal, 3 act Lewis signaling games with equiprobable states, we never observe total pooling equilibria, but we do see partial pooling between 4% and 5% of the time.[5] How is this possible? Are these simulations to be trusted?

There are four possible pairs of pure populations corresponding to values of 0 or 1 for x and y. Each of these population states is a dynamically unstable equilibrium.[6] But mixed populations, corresponding to non-extreme values of x and y, are all stable equilibria. Notice that in any of these states, signaling-system invaders would do worse against the natives than the natives do against themselves. Likewise for any other invaders. You can go through all of the other possible other sender and receiver strategies, and none of them do as well against a mixed pooling population as the poolers do against themselves. If you are close enough to the interior of the plane of partial pooling equilibria, the dynamics will lead you right into it. The simulations were a reliable guide. A non-trivial set of population proportions evolves by replicator dynamics to partial pooling rather than signaling systems.[7] In a perfectly ordinary Lewis signaling game, evolution can sometimes spontaneously create the synonyms and information bottlenecks that we artificially postulated in Chapter 1![8]

---

[5] Simulations using discrete time replicator dynamics by Kevin Zollman led to partial pooling in 4.7% of the trials, and to signaling systems the rest of the time.

[6] The instability stems from the fact that if a small number of senders and receivers that form the right signaling system were added they would out-compete the natives. They would do equally well against the natives, but better against each other. But each of these partial-pooling type populations requires a different signaling system to destabilize it, and each of these signaling systems does badly against the other type of partial-pooling.

[7] There are proofs of this in Huttegger 2007a and in Pawlowitsch 2008.

[8] Signals 2 and 3 function as synonyms, leaving only one signal for the remaining two states and two acts.

Mutation one more time

The set of partial pooling equilibria in the foregoing discussion is again an indication of *structural instability*. As before, let us try a little mutation. It is hard to do a full analysis of this game, but indications are that a little mutation destroys partial pooling and always gets us signaling. Partial pooling squares collapse to single points and move a little bit inward to accommodate a few mutants of other types. Although these equilibria of partial information transfer survive, they are dynamically unstable. Perturbed signaling systems, in contrast, are asymptotically stable attractors. Simulations using discrete-time replicator-mutator dynamics with both 1% and 0.1% mutation rates found that the system *always* converged to a (perturbed) signaling system equilibrium.

Correlation

In the last chapter, assortment of encounters made a cameo appearance. Assortment of encounters—that is, positive correlation of types in encounters—plays the major role in explanations of the evolution of altruism. Altruism, modeled as cooperation in the Prisoner's Dilemma, cannot evolve with random pairing. But it can when there is sufficient positive correlation of types, so that cooperators tend to meet cooperators and defectors tend to meet defectors.[9] Mechanisms exist in nature to promote an assortment of encounters. There is no reason to believe that they should operate only in Prisoner's Dilemma situations.

They can make a difference in evolution of signaling. Let us go back to a Lewis signaling game with two states, two signals, and two acts, where nature chooses state 1 with probability .2 and state 2 with

---

[9] See Hamilton 1964; Skyrms 1996; Bergstrom 2002.

EVOLUTION IN LEWIS SIGNALING GAMES 71

probability .8. Here we consider a one-population model, in which nature assigns roles of sender or receiver on flip of a fair coin. We focus on four strategies, written as a vector whose components are: signal sent in state 1, signal sent in state 2, act done after signal 1, act done after signal 2.

$$s1 = \langle 1, 2, 1, 2 \rangle$$
$$s2 = \langle 2, 1, 2, 1 \rangle$$
$$s3 = \langle 1, 1, 2, 2 \rangle$$
$$s4 = \langle 2, 2, 2, 2 \rangle$$

The first two strategies are signaling systems, the others are pooling strategies. (Other strategies neglected here are losers that rapidly go extinct.)

Consider the following model of assortment (due originally to Sewall Wright):

$$\text{Probability}(s_i \text{ meets } s_i) = p(s_i) + e[1 - p(s_i)]$$
$$\text{Probability}(s_i \text{ meets different } s_j) = p(s_j) - e\, p(s_j)$$

where p denotes population proportion. The probability of encountering your own type is augmented and that of encountering a different type is decremented. If $e = 1$, assortment is perfect; if $e = 0$ encounters are random.

Now consider the point, z, in the line of pooling equilibria where $p(s3) = p(s4) = .5$.

This point is stable. (It is, in fact, the point on the line with strongest resistance to invasion by signalers.) We feed in assortment. Between $e = .4$ and $e = .5$, z changes from being stable to unstable. This happens at about $e = .45$. If probabilities of states are more unequal, it takes greater correlation to destabilize pooling and guarantee the evolution of signaling. This is shown in figure 5.2. But if neither state is certain, there is always some degree of correlation that will do the trick.

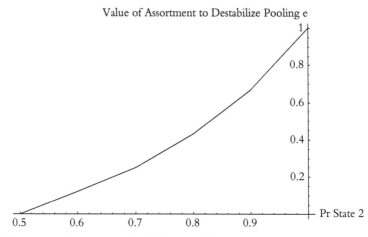

Value of Assortment to Destabilize Pooling e

Figure 5.2: Assortment destabilizes pooling.

This shows the power of correlation in the abstract. It remains to investigate the effect of specific correlation devices on the evolution of signaling.[10]

Eating crow

Even after all the good news is in, there remains a real possibility of evolution falling short of a signaling system. The emergence of a signaling system is not always a moral certainty. I was wrong. But signaling can still often emerge spontaneously, even though perfect signaling is not guaranteed to always emerge. Democritus is still right, but we can begin to see the nuance in how he is right.

[10] One correlation mechanism found widely in nature is local interaction in space, or in some social network structure. Wagner 2009 shows how network topology influences evolution of signaling systems.

6

Deception

"I can by no means will that lying should be a universal law.
For with such a law there would be no promises at all, since it
would be in vain to allege my intention in regard to my future
actions to those who would not believe this allegation . . . "

> Immanuel Kant, *Fundamental Principles*
> *of the Metaphysics of Morals*[1]

"the truth, the whole truth and nothing but the truth."

> Traditional in English Common Law

Is deception possible?

It seems like a silly question. Any theory that says that deception is
impossible is a non-starter. Deception is widespread enough in
human affairs, but it is not confined to our own species. Consider
the case of a low-ranking male vervet monkey, Kitui, reported by
Cheney and Seyfarth.[2] In intergroup encounters, Kitui gave false
leopard alarm calls when a new male attempted to transfer to his
group. But both groups became excited, ran up trees, and the

---

[1] Here is the full quotation, in the translation of Thomas Kingsmill Abbott: "I can by no
means will that lying should be a universal law. For with such a law there would be no
promises at all, since it would be in vain to allege my intention in regard to my future actions
to those who would not believe this allegation, or if they over hastily did so, would pay me
back in my own coin. Hence my maxim, as soon as it should be made a universal law, would
necessarily destroy itself" (Kant 1785).

[2] Cheney and Seyfarth 1990.

transfer never took place. You might wonder whether Kitui was just nervous, terribly afraid of leopards and prone to mistakes. If Kitui were just making mistakes, then his alarm calls were *misinformation*, but not deception. They were misinformation because the state was no leopard, and the probability of a leopard being present goes up given a leopard alarm call. Recalling Chapter 3, there is a positive quantity of information in the signal because it moves the probabilities of the state, but this use of the signal is *misinformation* because it decreases the probability of the true state and increases the probability of the false state. We suspect, however, that these are not simply mistakes because Kitui does this repeatedly and the results are to his own interest and against the interests of the receivers. If so, we appear to have a case of *deception*.

Nevertheless, biologists may worry about the stability of signaling systems in the presence of deception and philosophers sometimes wonder whether deception even makes sense in the context of a naturalistic theory of meaning. The philosophers, as usual, are more skeptical. According to their argument, a signal simply "means" *conditions are such as to cause this signal to be sent*. A signal cannot be false. Deception is impossible.

Systematic deception

One might be tempted to treat Kitui as an anomaly, an individual with non-standard payoffs who happens to wander into a well-established signaling system. If so, not much more needs to be said. But the use of systematic deceptive alarm calls has been documented in many species, both to drive others away from a newly discovered food source and—like Kitui—to deter sexual rivals.[3] These include birds and squirrels, who pose less of a temptation to anthropomorphism than monkeys. For two species of birds, great

---

[3] See Searcy and Nowicki 2005: ch. 6 for review and references.

tits and shrike tanagers, frequency of false alarm signals seems to be greater than that of true ones.

Or, if the temptation to imagine a mental life is still there with birds and squirrels, consider a somewhat different case of deception. Fireflies use their light for sexual signaling. In the western hemisphere, males fly over meadows, flashing a signal. If a female on the ground gives the proper sort of answering flashes, the male descends and they mate. The flashing "code" is species-specific. Females and males in general use and respond to the pattern of flashes only of their own species.

There is, however, an exception. A female firefly of the genus Photuris, when she observes a male of the genus Photinus, may mimic the female signals of the male's species, lure him in, and eat him. She gets not only a nice meal, but also some useful protective chemicals that she cannot get in any other way. One species, *Photuris versicolor*, is a remarkably accomplished mimic—capable of sending the appropriate flash patterns of 11 Photinus species. I would say that this qualifies as deception, wouldn't you?

Let us think about this, not in terms of some propositional content imputed to the signal, but in terms of its informational content. We consider the probabilities of the states, and the probabilities of the states conditional on the signal being sent.[4] In the case of the false alarm call, the probability of there being a predator present conditional on the alarm call being sent is higher than the unconditional probability. It is not equal to one, and may not even be close to one, due to what we have called systematic deception. But the signal still raises this probability.

If the signal is sent in a situation where the sender observes no predator, it is *misinformation*. If, in addition, it is systematically sent to the benefit of the sender and the detriment of the receiver, it is *deception*.[5]

---

[4] As in Chapter 3.
[5] One could argue over whether the clause about the detriment of the receiver should be included. Searcy and Nowicki 2005: 5 leave it out:

Likewise, the sexual predator Photuris sends a signal that raises the probability of the state of a sexually receptive female being present when that is not the true state. This is just a question of actual frequencies. There is a frequency of receptive females being present and there is a frequency of receptive females in situations where the mating signal is given. The second frequency is higher than the first. As a consequence, the receiving males are led to actions that they would not take if they could directly observe the state.

The signal carries misinformation.

Signals carrying misinformation might sometimes result from mistakes. For instance, we might suppose that occasionally a sexually receptive female of another species gets her flash pattern mixed up and sends the appropriate signal for Photinus. But Photuris is not making a mistake; she is getting dinner. This is a systematic use of misinformation to manipulate the behavior of the receiver for the advantage of the sender.

This is deception.

Half-truth

But the firefly mating signal also increases the probability of the presence of a predator. Its informational content is mixed. Let us look at the matter a little more closely. When a cruising Photinus

---

we will define deception as occurring when:

1. A receiver registers something Y from a signaler;
2. The receiver responds in such a way that
   a. Benefits the signaler and
   b. Is appropriate if Y means X; and
3. It is not true that X is the case.

Maynard Smith and Harper 2003: 86 put it in.

I do not think that much hangs on the choice; we could talk about strong and weak deception. What is important is that our definition is information-based, rather than depending on imputed propositional content that is false. Imputation of propositional content to animal signals is always problematic. It might make a limited amount of sense in a favorable equilibrium. The information-based concept, however, always makes sense—both in and out of equilibrium.

looks for an opportunity to mate, nature chooses among three states: sexually receptive Photinus present, hungry Photuris present, nothing happening. Photinus can receive one of two signals, the mating signal or the null signal (that is, no real signal).

This is a little different from the models we have considered, but the same way of thinking of information about states can be applied. There is a baseline frequency for each of the states. There are frequencies when the signal is sent. We can assume for simplicity that in the first two states the mating signal is always sent and the third always leads to the null signal. Then the mating signal being sent raises the probability of both kinds of partner, but leaves the ratio unchanged. If you want to think of it as saying "I am the kind who sends this signal," you can think of it as telling the truth. But it is only a half-truth.

When sent by the predator it contains misinformation in that it raises the probability that a sexually receptive partner is available. When sent by the potential mate, it also contains misinformation, because it raises the probability of a predator. But only the first case counts as *deception* because only in this case does the sender profit at the expense of the receiver. A half-truth can be a form of deception.

Where deception is impossible

Let's just change the payoff structure from common interest to diametrically opposed interest in our simplest signaling game. Nature chooses between two states with equal probability; the sender chooses between two signals; the receiver chooses between two acts. But now the receiver gets paid when the act matches the state, and the sender gets paid when it doesn't.

The only equilibria in this game are *pooling equilibria*. If the signals gave the receiver information about the state, the receiver could exploit the sender. If the receiver altered her behavior in response to the signal she could be manipulated by the sender.

Deception is impossible because the signals carry no information at all. The probability of each state (and of each act) being given a signal is equal to its unconditional probability. The informational content vectors are all full of zeros; the quantity of information about states (and about acts) in each signal is zero; the information flow is nonexistent.

That is only in equilibrium. A lot of life is lived out of equilibrium. If receivers tend to do act one for signal one and act two for signal two, then senders can profit by deceiving receivers. If senders tend to send signal two in state 1 and conversely, then receivers can improve their lot by learning to read the information in senders' signals—that is, by adjusting their strategies to turn misinformation into useful information. Deception is one of the forces that drive the system to equilibrium.

That is, if the system goes to equilibrium. It may not. Consider our game with strategies restricted to signaling strategies. The sender sends a different signal in each state, and the receiver does a different act for each signal. There are now only two sender's strategies and two receiver's strategies. Payoffs are:

	Receiver 1	Receiver 2
Sender 2	1, 0	0, 1
Sender 1	0, 1	1, 0

With two populations, the population proportions live on a square, with the x axis being the proportion of receivers playing their strategy two, and the y axis being the proportion of senders playing their strategy 2. With the replicator dynamics we see cycles, rather than convergence to equilibrium, as shown in figure 6.1.

In the top half of the square the sender strategy 1 conveys misinformation. In each state, its signals move the probability of the state off ½ in the wrong direction because of the prevalence in sender strategy 2. Likewise, in the bottom half of the

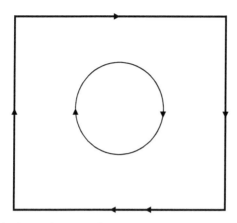

Figure 6.1: Cycles with opposed interests.

square, strategy 2 conveys misinformation. Sender strategy 1 profits at the expense of receivers, on average, in the right half of the square and sender strategy 2 is systematically profitable in the left half. So, according to our definition, deception predominates in the upper right and lower left quadrants. Sender's deception and receiver's adaptations drive the cycle round and round. (The same phenomenon can be realized in a single population, where the payoffs have a rock-scissors-paper structure.)

Prevalence of deception

Consider standard sender-receiver signaling games with all sorts of payoffs. Cases of pure common interest and of pure conflict are the extremes. As the number of states, signals and acts grows, and as dyadic interactions give way to networks, the pure extreme cases become less and less likely. What is typical is a case of mixed interests, in some combination of partial alignment and partial divergence. From purely abstract considerations, what we should expect to predominate is some combination of information and misinformation.[6]

That is what we find. In all kinds of signaling systems in nature there is information transmission which is sufficient to maintain signaling, but we also find misinformation and even deception. After an extensive review of models of animal signals and of the relevant empirical evidence bearing on these models, Searcy and Nowicki conclude "Evidence supporting the occurrence of deception has been found in all the major categories of signaling systems that we have discussed, including begging, alarming, mating signals and aggressive signals."[7]

How is deception possible?

We have been able to characterize misinformation and deception in behavioral terms. Despite some misgivings in the philosophical literature,[8] misinformation is straightforward. If receipt of a signal moves probabilities of states it contains information about the state. If it moves the probability of a state in the wrong direction—either by diminishing the probability of the state in which it is sent, or raising the probability of a state other than the one in which it is sent—then it is misleading information, or *misinformation*. If misinformation is sent systematically and benefits the sender at the expense of the receiver, we will not shrink from following the biological literature in calling it *deception*.

In certain cases of diametrically opposed interests it is impossible, as Kant says, for everyone to practice deception, at least in equilibrium. That is because, in equilibrium, there is no information at all in the signals. In a game with partially aligned interests it may be in the interest of a sender to restrict information to manipulate a

[6] See Crawford and Sobel 1982.

[7] Searcy and Nowicki 2005: 223.

[8] For a review of the philosophical literature on this subject and commentary see Godfrey-Smith 1989.

receiver and it may nevertheless be in the interest of a receiver to act on the information that she gets. Consider the following payoffs (for equiprobable states):

	Act 1	Act 2	Act 3
State 1	2, 10	0, 0	10, 8
State 2	0, 0	2, 10	10, 8
State 3	0, 0	10, 10	0, 0

If everyone uses the strategy, *If sender send signal 1 in states 1 and 2 and signal 2 in state 3; if receiver do act 3 on receipt of signal 1 and act 2 on receipt of signal, 2* the situation is an equilibrium. In this equilibrium, the occupant of the sender's role always manipulates the occupant of the receiver's role. In state one, the sender's signal is a half-truth in that it raises the probability of state 2. In state 2 the sender's signal is a half-truth in that it raises the probability of state 1. These half-truths induce the receiver to choose act 3 in states 1 and 2, whereas accurate knowledge of the state would lead her to choose either act 1 or act 2. The manipulation leads to a greater payoff for the sender and a smaller one for the receiver. In this sense, universal deception in equilibrium is indeed possible.

It might be objected that this is not *universal* deception because if nature chooses state 3, the signal sent is not deceptive. We have universal strategies that incorporate deception, but not universal deception. The objection can be met by simply expanding the game so there is an equilibrium in which state 3 is pooled with a new state 4:

	Act 1	Act 2	Act 3	Act 4
State 1	2, 10	0, 0	10, 8	0, 0
State 2	0, 0	2, 10	10, 8	0, 0
State 3	2, 10	0, 0	0, 0	10, 8
State 4	0, 0	2, 10	0, 0	10, 8

Now it would be in the receiver's best advantage to do act 1 in states 1 and 3 and act 2 in states 2 and 4. But there is an equilibrium in which the sender sends one signal in both states 1 and 2 and another in both states 3 and 4, and the receiver does act 3 upon receiving the first signal and act 4 on receiving the second. Given the information supplied, the receiver behaves optimally, preferring a sure payoff of 8 to a 50% chance of 10. The sender has manipulated the receiver to assure herself a payoff of 10. Every signal sent in this equilibrium is deceptive.

Universal deception in this strong sense is not only *logically* consistent in the sense of involving no contradiction, but also *evolutionarily* consistent in the sense of being an equilibrium. I would remind those who would insist that deception is a matter of intentions, that the equilibrium is also *consistent with rational choice*. Sender and receiver may be perfectly aware of what is going on and be perfectly rational and still intend to do what they are doing.

Kant was wrong, wasn't he? (At least if half-truths count as deceptions.) Well, you might say, he was wrong to think that there was an actual inconsistency involved but right that you cannot will deception to be a universal law. For wouldn't our players prefer a system in which the signals carry perfect information about the states? They would not.

If it were a universal law that the senders' signals identify the states and that the receivers choose the act that is best response to that information, the outcomes are those italicized in the payoff table. Compare these with the deceptive equilibrium, whose outcomes are shown in boldface. If one is in the role of sender half the time and that of receiver half the time, the average payoff with honest signaling is 6 and that for deception is 9. Deception is good for you. You would choose the deceptive equilibrium as universal law.

Well, perhaps Kant is not talking about this game, but about all games. You cannot (rationally) will deception to be universal law in all games. Fair enough. But our example shows that one can not rationally will honest signaling to be a universal law either. That is my point. If we concentrate on a few extreme cases, we miss a lot of what is important in communication.

7

Learning

"Of several responses made to the same situation, those
which are accompanied or closely followed by satisfaction
to the animal will, other things being equal, be more firmly
connected with the situation, so that, when it recurs, they will
be more likely to recur."

Edward Thorndike, *Animal Intelligence*, 1911

The Law of Effect

When Edward Thorndike, as an undergraduate English major at
Wesleyan University, read William James' *Principles of Psychology*,
he switched his interests. After graduating in 1895 he moved to
Harvard, and eventually conducted learning experiments on chickens in the basement of William James' house. The epigraph to
this chapter is a statement of Thorndike's famous "Law of Effect,"
taken from his 1911 *Animal Intelligence*.

Despite Thorndike's high regard for James, his studies of what is
now known as reinforcement learning were a move away from
introspective cognitive psychology towards a theory more focused
on behavior. In the spirit of Darwin, he focused on commonalities
between human and animals. That this focus sometimes generated a

certain amount of hostility is evident from his introductory para-
graph of an article on the law of effect:[1]

It (*the Law of Effect*) has been even more odious to philosophers and
educational theorists, who find it a dangerous antagonist to, or an inferior
substitute for, their explanations of behavior by purposes . . .

We think that investigation of reinforcement learning is a complement to the study of belief learning, rather than being a "dangerous
antagonist." Our strategy will be to begin at the low end of the
scale, to see how far simple reinforcement learning can get us, and
then move up. Exactly how does degree of reinforcement affect the
strengthening of the bond between stimulus and response? Different answers are possible, and these give us alternative theories of the
law of effect.

Roth–Erev reinforcement

In 1995 Al Roth and Ido Erev used a version of reinforcement
learning to account for how subjects actually behave in experiments.[2] The experiments have the subjects repeatedly playing a
game, and sophisticated rational choice fails to explain the experimental data. Roth and Erev, following pioneering early investiga-
tions by Patrick Suppes and Richard Atkinson show that
reinforcement gives a much better explanation.[3]

Roth and Erev's basic model works like this. The probability of
choosing an action is proportional to the total accumulated rewards
from choosing it in the past. They trace the idea back to the
psychologist Richard Herrnstein.[4] Some initial equal inclinations,

[1] Thorndike 1927.
[2] Roth and Erev 1995; Erev and Roth 1998.
[3] Suppes and Atkinson 1960.
[4] Herrnstein 1961, 1970.

or propensities, are assumed to get the process started by choosing at random.[5]

We can visualize the operation of the law of effect in terms of drawing balls from an urn. For instance, suppose you have two actions and start out with an urn containing one red and one black ball. On the first trial, you draw a ball and choose act 1 if it is red and act 2 if it is black. Suppose you choose act 1 and get a reward of two. Then you put two more red balls in the urn and draw again. Now the chance of drawing a black ball is 1/4. But suppose you draw the one black ball and get a reward of six. Then you put in six black balls, and draw again. In this way the urn keeps track of accumulated rewards. We don't really need an urn. Organisms may keep track of accumulated rewards by strength of neural connections,[6] or concentrations of pheromones,[7] or any number of ways.

We can summarize the basic Roth–Erev reinforcement process as follows: (i) there are some initial inclination weights; (ii) weights evolve by addition of rewards gotten; (iii) probability of choosing an alternative is proportional to the inclination weights.

When the magnitudes of the rewards are fixed, there is only one parameter of the process. That is the magnitude of the initial equal weights. If they are very large, learning starts off very slowly. If they are small, initially probabilities can move a lot. But either way, as reinforcements pile up, individual trials can move probabilities less and less. Learning slows down. In psychology, the qualitative phenomenon of learning slowing down in this way is called the *Law of Practice*.

---

[5] Later on, we will also consider variations of the process where the initial propensities are unequal.

[6] For a summary of what is known of the neurology, see Schultz 2004.

[7] The pheromones in food trails of ants act as a transient record of food obtained that is essentially a reinforcement memory stored outside the individual ants. Evaporation of the pheromone strongly discounts the past so that if it is not continually reinforced the trail vanishes. See Hölldobler and Wilson 1990.

Bush–Mosteller Reinforcement

In 1950 Bush and Mosteller suggested a different realization of the law of effect. Today's rewards act directly on probabilities of acts— there is no memory of accumulated reinforcements. The most basic model looks like this: If an act is chosen and a reward is gotten the probability is incremented by adding some fraction of the distance between the original probability and probability one.[8] Alternative action probabilities are decremented so that everything adds to one. The fraction used is the product of the reward and some learning parameter. Rewards are scaled to lie in the interval from zero to one, and the learning parameter is some fraction.

For example, suppose that there are just two actions and the current probability of act one is .6. Suppose that you happen to choose act 1 and get a reward of 1. Take the learning parameter to be .1, then your new probability of act one is $.6 + .1 \, (1-.6) = .64$. Your new probability of act 2 is .36. At this point the learning parameter is the only parameter. If it is small you learn slowly; if it is larger, you learn fast. But learning does not slow down as it does in Roth–Erev reinforcement. Basic Bush–Mosteller does not obey the Law of Practice.

Bush–Mosteller learning has also been used to explain empirical data.[9] Both Roth–Erev reinforcement and Bush–Mosteller reinforcement have led to versions with various modifications and lots of parameters, but for now we stick with the simplest versions of each. We would like to compare them. In the long run they can behave quite differently.

---

[8] The dynamics may be more familiar in the form of updating with a weighted average of the old probability and some maximum attainable probability, which I here take to be 1. Thus, if A is tried and the product of the reward gotten and the learning parameter is α, then $\mathrm{pr}_{new}(A) = (1-\alpha)\,\mathrm{pr}_{old}(A) + \alpha\,(1)$. This is equivalent to $\mathrm{pr}_{new}(A) = \mathrm{pr}_{old}(A) + \alpha\,(1-\mathrm{pr}_{old}(A))$, which is the way I said it in the text.

[9] Macy 1991; Flache and Macy 2002; Macy and Flache 2002; Borgers and Sarin 2000.

Slot machines and medical trials

Consider two slot machines that pay off at different unknown rates—or alternatively, different drugs with different unknown probabilities of successful treatment. A trial-and-error learner has to balance two different considerations. She doesn't want to lock onto the wrong machine just because it got lucky in a few initial trials. But nor does she want to explore forever, and never learn to play the optimal machine. Likewise, in medical research we don't want to *jump to conclusions*. We want to explore long enough to have a valid study. But if one treatment is clearly better, we don't want to deny it to those who need it by dithering about. There is a tension between gaining knowledge and using it. As John Holland put it in 1975,[10] there is a tradeoff between exploration and exploitation.

If our gambler sometimes freezes into always playing the wrong machine, we will say her version of reinforcement is *too cold*. She learns too fast. If she gets stuck in exploring, and never learns to play one machine, even in the limit, we will say that her version of reinforcement is *too hot*. She never fully learns. Goldilocks reinforcement learning would be neither too hot nor too cold.[11] It would always converge to playing the optimal machine with probability one. In the drug trials model, it would always learn to use the best treatment.

Is there Goldilocks reinforcement learning? In 2005, Alan Beggs proved that Roth–Erev reinforcement has the Goldilocks

---

[10] Holland 1975.
[11] The reference is to the tale of Goldilocks and the Three Bears:

At the table in the kitchen, there were three bowls of porridge. Goldilocks was hungry. She tasted the porridge from the first bowl. "This porridge is too hot!" she exclaimed. So, she tasted the porridge from the second bowl. "This porridge is too cold," she said. So, she tasted the last bowl of porridge. "Ahhh, this porridge is just right," she said happily and she ate it all up.

property.[12] The theorem was already proved in this context in 1978, by Wei and Durham[13]—using different mathematical techniques.

Bush–Mosteller learning, as presented above, is too cold. It can freeze into playing the worse slot machine. This is because Bush–Mosteller reinforcement does not slow down with more practice. It learns too fast.[14]

Reinforcement and evolution

Reinforcement learning is probabilistic; at any juncture alternative acts may be selected and alternative paths taken. But inside the probabilistic process lies a deterministic dynamics describing the expected motion at every point in the process.

This is called the average, or mean-field dynamics.[15] If learning is very slow—if it proceeds in tiny steps—then with high probability the real learning path will, for some time, approximate the mean-field dynamics. So it is of some interest to ask what this mean-field dynamics is for our two basic models of reinforcement learning.

In 1997 Tilman Börgers and Rajiv Sarin showed that the mean-field dynamics for Bush–Mosteller learning is a version of the replicator dynamics. In 2005, Alan Beggs and also Ed Hopkins and Martin Posch showed that the mean-field dynamics of Roth–Erev learning is a version of the replicator dynamics. In Chapter 1, we started with one question and ended up with two: *How can*

[12] Beggs used stochastic approximation theory, which will enter again later in this chapter. In stochastic approximation theory, the Goldilocks property has a precise characterization (connected with decreasing step size of order $1/n$). Beggs 2005; Pemantle 2007.

[13] Wei and Durham 1978.

[14] Some fancier versions of Bush–Mosteller with dynamically adjusting aspiration levels can be too hot. They may exhibit some degree of "probability matching" and never converge to one machine. See Borgers and Sarin 2000.

[15] For any state of the learner, various things can happen with various probabilities leading by stochastic dynamics to a new state. Some state is the probability weighted average of the possible new states, or the expected new state. The deterministic dynamics that maps any state onto the expected new state of the stochastic dynamics is called the associated mean-field dynamics.

interacting individuals spontaneously learn to signal? How can species spontaneously evolve signaling systems? Now we see that these two questions are closely intertwined.[16]

Why then, are the dynamics so different in the long run? The key is that the Roth–Erev dynamics slows down in such a way that replicator dynamics is a good indication of limiting behavior.[17] Bush–Mosteller does not slow down, so while it may be likely to stay close to replicator dynamics for a finite stretch of time, it may not be close at all in the long run. There is a theory of slowing down in such a way that the mean-field dynamics is a good guide to limiting behavior, the theory of stochastic approximation.[18] This is the theory that Beggs used to prove that Roth–Erev learning has the Goldilocks property in medical trials and the slot machine problem. As we shall see in the next chapter, it is also the tool for analyzing this kind of reinforcement in signaling games.[19]

Variations on reinforcement

Both of the realizations of the law of effect that we have discussed have given rise to various modified versions. Negative payoffs have been considered, with the zero point either fixed or itself evolving. Errors have been introduced. A little bit of forgetting the past has been introduced into the Roth–Erev model (Bush–Mosteller already forgets the past.) Different ways of translating inclination weights into choice probabilities have been tried with Roth–Erev.

One popular approach is to use an *exponential response rule*. The basic idea is to make probabilities proportional to the exponential of

---

[16] Indeed, some models of evolution in a finite population are remarkably similar to the Roth–Erev model of reinforcement learning. Payoffs are in offspring, and offspring are just individuals of the same type. The difference is that individuals die at random, so with some bad luck types (or even the whole population) may go extinct. But if this doesn't happen and the population grows, then the probabilistic process approximates the replicator dynamics just as reinforcement learning does. Shreiber 2001; Benaim, Shreiber, and Tarres 2004.

[17] Of necessity, there is a little over-simplification here.

[18] Benaim 1999; Pemantle 1990, 2007.

[19] Argiento et al. 2009.

past reinforcements.[20] Or more generally, past reinforcements are multiplied by some constant, lambda, and probabilities are proportional to the exponential. In analogy with thermodynamics, the reciprocal of lambda is sometimes called the temperature. If lambda is zero the temperature is infinite, and everything is tried with equal probability. If lambda is large, the act with the largest accumulated rewards is chosen with high probability. Starting with a high temperature and slowly cooling off is called *simulated annealing*, which has been shown to have nice properties for exploring a fixed environment. The effect of rewards piling up in Roth–Erev reinforcement, modified with the exponential response rule, is to slowly cool off the system.

Belief and decision

Reinforcement learners do not have to know their opponent's payoffs; they do not have to know the structure of the game. If acts are reinforced, they do not have to know that they *are* in a game. But now we will move up a level. Individuals know that they are in a game. They know the structure of the game. They know how the combination of others' actions and their own affect their payoffs. They can observe actions of all the players in repeated plays of the game. They can think about all this.

New possibilities for learning now open up. Individuals form beliefs from past experience about how others are likely to act. They then use these beliefs and their knowledge of the game to decide what to do. Different varieties of belief learning dynamics arise from different accounts of how beliefs are formed and different ways of reaching decisions.

---

[20] See, for instance, Blume et al. 2002 for an experimental study of signaling games that evaluates reinforcement learning with an exponential response rule. They, somewhat misleadingly, call this Roth–Erev reinforcement, but it differs from the Roth and Erev model in the response rule.

The very simplest way to form beliefs is to just assume that others will do the same thing that they did last time. The most straightforward way to choose is to pick the best for you, given your beliefs. The combination is called the *best response dynamics*.

It was first studied in the nineteenth century by the mathematician, philosopher and economist Antoine Augustin Cournot.[21] For this reason it is sometimes called *Cournot dynamics*.

Inductive logic

The foregoing uses an almost laughably simple method of belief formation. With a history of past play, it would be possible to form beliefs by Bayesian inductive logic. The simplest Bayesian model treats the others as flips of a coin, or rolls of a die, with unknown bias. This gives us *Laplace's rule of succession*. If you choose the best response to these beliefs, the resulting dynamics is, for the following odd historical reason, known as *fictitious play*. In the very early days of game theory, it was thought that a good way to find equilibria in games would be to program one of the (then new) computers to simulate the play of actual players—thus *fictitious play*. The model of the learning dynamics of the players that was suggested at the time by G. B. Brown in 1951 is essentially that just described.[22]

There are a variety of learning models that interpolate between pure reinforcement learning and fictitious play,[23] and experimental studies that fit them to experimental data.[24]

---

[21] Cournot had his players, who were two duopolists controlling a market, alternate best responses. One might vary the dynamics by having the players best-respond at random times, and just keep doing the same thing otherwise. This is called *best response with inertia*.

[22] Brown 1951. A lot has been learned about the properties of fictitious play since it was introduced. For a review see Fudenberg and Levine 1998.

[23] See Fudenberg and Levine 1998 and Camerer and Ho 1999.

[24] In the short run it may be hard to discriminate between these models. See Salmon 2001.

Learning to signal

In Chapter 1, we articulated the strategy of starting with reinforcement learning and moving up to belief learning only if reinforcement learning fails. There was a dual rationale for this approach. First, a positive result for reinforcement learning would apply not just to humans, but also to many sorts of animals. Second, reinforcement learning was supposed to be a worst-case scenario. If it allowed us to learn to signal, surely more sophisticated forms of learning would do so too. Is that right? It is time to take a look.

8

Learning in Lewis Signaling Games

Can we learn to signal? Obviously we can and do. We are not the only species able to do this, although others may not do it so well. The real question is what is required to be able to learn to signal. Or, better, *what kind of learning is capable of spontaneously generating signaling?* If the learning somehow has the signaling system prepro-gramed in, then learning to signal is not very interesting. If the learning mechanism is general purpose and low level, learning to signal is quite interesting. In Chapter 1, we saw that for one kind of signaling game, low level reinforcement learning could learn to signal. If many kinds of low level learning allow the spontaneous emergence of signaling in many situations, we are on the way to a robust explanation.

Roth–Erev reinforcement

We return to two-state, two-signal, and two-act games with states equiprobable, and put in all possible strategies. There are now an infinite number of pooling equilibria, as well as the signaling systems. We would most like an analysis of this case where rein-forcement operates not on whole strategies, but rather on individual acts. Then agents would not even need to see the situations they find themselves in as part of a single game.

Suppose that the sender has a separate set of inclination weights—of accumulated past reinforcements—for each state of the world. You can think of each state as coming equipped with its own urn, with balls of different colors for different signals to send. The receiver has a separate set of accumulated reinforcements for each signal. You can think of the receiver as having a different urn for each signal received, with balls of different colors for different acts to choose.

Spontaneous emergence of signaling in this more challenging set-up would be fully consonant with the spirit of Democritus, "who sets the world at chance."[1] It requires no strategic reasoning, just chance and reinforcement. This is, in fact, just what happens. Individuals *always* learn to signal in the long run. This is not only confirmed by extensive simulations, it is also a theorem.[2] In this situation individuals converge to a signaling system with probability one, with the two possible signaling systems being equally likely. Spontaneous emergence of signaling is virtually guaranteed.

That is limiting behavior, but what of the short run? Figure 8.1 shows the results of simulations starting with initial weights all equal to 1. Learning is fast. On average, after 100 trials individuals have an 80% success rate. After 300 trials they are right 90% of the time.

---

[1] As Dante has him in the Divine Comedy, Canto IV:

> Then when a little more I rais'd my brow,
> I spied the master of the sapient throng,
> Seated amid the philosophic train.
> Him (*Aristotle*) all admire, all pay him rev'rence due.
> There Socrates and Plato both I mark'd,
> Nearest to him in rank; Democritus,
> Who sets the world at chance, Diogenes,
> With Heraclitus, and Empedocles,
> And Anaxagoras, and Thales sage,
> Zeno, and Dioscorides well read
> In nature's secret lore.

I would put Democritus higher.

[2] Argiento et al. 2009.

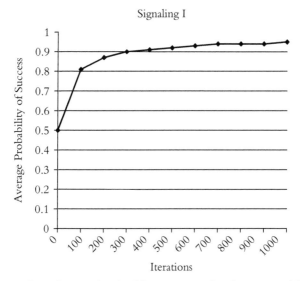

Figure 8.1: Learning to signal with 2 states, 2 signals, 2 acts with states equiprobable. Initial weights =1. Reinforcements for success=1.

Harder cases

Does the bad news about the replicator dynamics carry over as well as the good news? Does reinforcement learning sometimes learn partial-pooling (with only partial information transfer) in Lewis games with three states, three signals, and three acts? And does it sometimes end up in total pooling (with no information transfer) where there are only two states, signals and acts, and the states have unequal probabilities?

A full analytic treatment of these questions is not available. But they can be investigated by simulation. We will concentrate on reinforcing acts. There is only one parameter of the reinforcement, the initial weights with which we start the process. For the purpose of initial simulations, we start each player with an *initial weight of one* for each possible choice, players choose with probability proportional to their weights, and we augment weights by *adding a payoff of one* for a success. In Lewis signaling games with three equiprobable states, three signals and three acts, reinforcement learning learns to signal in a little more than 90% of trials, but lands on partial pooling in the rest. As the number of states, signals and acts increases the success rate goes down. If the number is 4, simulations hit signaling a little less than 80%; if the number is 8, perfect signaling emerges less than half the time.[3]

And even in the basic game where the number of states, signals and acts is 2, unequal probability of the states can sometimes lead to signals that contain no information at all. How often depends on the magnitude of the inequality. When one state has probability .6, suboptimal outcomes hardly ever happen, at probability .7 they happen 5% of the time. This number rises to 22% for probability .8, and 44% for probability .9.[4] Suboptimal equilibria are still there.

Roth and Erev found their learning relatively insensitive to initial choice of weights, but they were considering a different class of games. So we should try varying the weight parameter. We set the probabilities of states quite unequal, at 90%–10% and run reinforcement dynamics with initial weights of different orders of magnitude. The probability of ending up in pooling equilibrium instead of a signaling system is shown in the figure 8.2.

Initial weights make an enormous difference! If we raise them to 10, then the probability of getting trapped in a pooling equilibrium goes up to 94%. If we lower them to .01 probability of pooling goes down to 1%. And at the minuscule initial weights of .0001, we saw no pooling at all; each trial led to a signaling system.[5] The one innocuous parameter of Roth–Erev learning becomes crucial. Small initial weights also lead to signaling in larger Lewis signaling games.

How are they performing their magic? The explanation cannot come near the end of the learning process. There the initial

[3] Barrett 2006.

[4] These simulations are for 1000 trials, with 100,000 iterations of reinforcement learning on each trial.

[5] At state one probabilities of .8, .7, and .6 we always get signaling for initial propensities .0001, and .001.

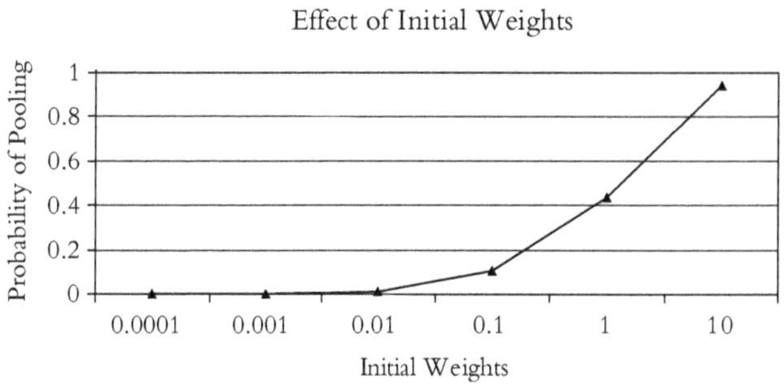

Effect of Initial Weights

Figure 8.2: Effect of initial weights where state probabilities are 90%–10%.

weights, whether great or small, have been swamped by reinforce-ment. Rather, small initial weights must have their impact at the beginning of the learning process, where they make the initial probabilities easy to modify. Perhaps the explanation is that they both facilitate initial exploration and enhance sensitivity to success.

Bush–Mosteller reinforcement

In the simplest Lewis signaling game with equiprobable states, it was proved that Roth–Erev learners would learn to signal with probability one. In the proof, it is crucial that Roth–Erev learners do not learn too fast or too slowly. They are neither too hot nor too cold. This is no longer true for reinforcement learners who learn according to the basic dynamics of Bush and Mosteller. The basic Bush–Mosteller learning dynamics is too cold. Sometimes it freezes into suboptimal states.[6] This is not to say, however, that Bush–Mosteller learners never learn to signal. To get an indication of how often they learn successfully, and how fast, we turn to simulations.

---

[6] Hopkins and Posch 2005; Borgers and Sarin 1997; Izquierdo et al. 2007.

The surprising result is that, despite the theoretical possibilities for unhappy outcomes, Bush–Mosteller learners are very successful indeed. The only parameter of the learning dynamics is the learning rate, which is between zero and one. In our basic signaling game, for a wide range of learning rates between .05 and .5, individuals learned to signal in at least 99.9% of the trials. These results are from running simulations out to 10,000 iterations of the learning process. For the short run, consider just 300 iterations of learning. With the learning parameter at .1, then in 95% of the trials individuals had already learned to signal with a success rate of more than 98%. Learning to signal is no longer guaranteed, but it is still to be strongly expected.

What of the more problematic cases, in which states have un-equal probabilities?

Here, variations in the learning parameter can make a big differ-ence, just as variations in the magnitudes of the initial weights did in Roth–Erev reinforcement. For comparison with figure 8.2, we reconsider the case in which the state probabilities are 90%–10%. using Bush–Mosteller.[7]

With a high enough learning parameter, we reliably learn to signal even with highly unequal state probabilities. If we concentrate on the short and medium run, the situation with

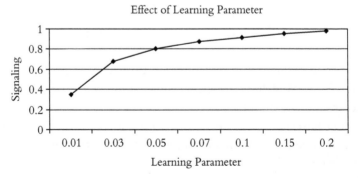

Figure 8.3: Effect of learning parameter with state probabilities 90%–10%.

[7] 1,000 trials, 100,000 iterations per trial.

Bush–Mosteller reinforcement doesn't look much different from that of Roth–Erev reinforcement.

Exponential response

Consider Roth–Erev modified by using an exponential response rule. Choice probabilities are no longer simply proportional to weights, but rather to:

$$\mathrm{Exp}[\lambda * \mathrm{weight}].$$

The constant λ controls the noise in the response probabilities. When $\lambda = 0$, noise washes out all other considerations, and all possible choices are equally probable. When λ is high, the rule almost always picks the alternative with the highest weight.

The exponential response rule interacts with cumulative reinforcements of propensities in an interesting way. As propensities grow, the learner moves more and more towards a sure pick of the alternative with the highest propensity. If we start with a very small λ, we start with lots of random exploration that gradually moves towards deterministic choice.[8]

In two-state Lewis signaling games with unequal state probabilities (probability of state one at .6, .7, .8, .9), simulations of this learning model with small λ (.0001 to .01) always converge to signaling systems.[9] Similar results are gotten for three-state Lewis games.[10] The range of values is not implausible for human learning.

---

[8] For example, suppose the choice is between two acts, A and B and that A is reinforced three times for every two times B is reinforced. Let lambda in the exponential response rule be .001, the propensity for A be 3n, and the propensity for B, 2n. Then for n=10 the probability to choose A would be .5025 — just a little more than one half. But for n=100 this probability would be .5250; for n=1000, .7311; for n=10,000, .999955. Since the ratio of the responses has been kept constant at three to two in this example, the linear response rule would have kept probability of A at 2/3.

[9] This is not true for larger values of λ.

[10] The mechanism is somewhat different from that in win-stay, lose-randomize.

This form of reinforcement learning allows individuals to avoid suboptimal equilibria and to arrive at efficient information transfer.

More Complex Reinforcement

There are all sorts of refinements and variations of the foregoing models. Yoella Bereby-Meyer and Ido Erev[11] compare models and conclude that a modification of Roth–Erev learning, which they call the ARP model, best fits the data. This model incorporates negative payoffs, which result in balls being taken out of the urn, and a floating reference point, which determines which payoffs are positive or negative. Payoffs above the reference point are positive, those below are negative, and the reference point itself adjusts in response to past experience. In good times your reference floats up, in bad times it settles down. What you are used to eventually tends to become your reference point. Negative payoffs are subtracted from weights until they are almost equal to zero.

The point where we stop subtracting is called the truncation point. There is a little discounting of the past. There are errors. All of these modifications have psychological currency. This is a model with a lot of parameters. Erev and Bereby-Meyer fit the parameters to the data.

Jeffrey Barrett has taken the ARP model, together with the parameter values gotten from the data by Erev and Bereby-Meyer, and shown how this type of learning allows one to learn to signal.[12] Barrett finds that the basic modifications introduced into the model for psychological reasons tend to make it easier to learn to signal.[13] I believe that at this point we can conclude that the

[11] Bereby-Meyer and Erev 1998.

[12] Barrett 2006, 2007a, 2007b. Barrett and Zollman 2007.

[13] There are other competing complex models with their own parameters to estimate from the data. It would be nice to have a definitive realistic model to apply to signaling. At this time there seems to be no clear winner. The models all fit the data reasonably well. Salmon 2001; Feltovich 2000; Erev and Haruvy 2005.

possibility of learning to signal by simple reinforcement is a reasonably robust finding.

Neural Nets

Patrick Grim, Paul St. Denis, and Trina Kokalis[14] consider spontaneous emergence of signaling in neural nets. There is a spatial array of agents, each equipped with a neural net. Both food sources and predators migrate through space. There are different optimal actions—feed or hide—in the presence of a food source or a predator. Individuals can utter potential signals that are received (taken as inputs) by their neighbors.

Periodically, individuals have their neural nets "trained up" by their most successful neighbors. Simulations show spontaneous emergence of successful signaling in which individuals "warn" of predators in the neighborhood and "advertise" wandering food sources.

Imitating neighbors

Kevin Zollman also investigates learning to signal by interaction with neighbors on a spatial grid, using imitation dynamics.[15] Each individual looks at eight neighbors, to the N, NE, E, SE, S, SW, W, NW, and imitates the most successful neighbor if that neighbor does better than she does. Ties are broken at random. He considers two games. The first is a Lewis signaling game with two states, acts, and signals. Signaling evolves. In 10,000 simulations, starting with a random assignment of strategies, signaling systems always emerged. However, alternative signaling systems coexisted, each occupying

---

[14] Grim et al. 2002.
[15] Zollman 2005.

different areas. We see spontaneous generation of regional signaling dialects.

His second game is even more interesting. Signaling is possible prior to playing another game—the Stag Hunt—with neighbors. Play in the Stag Hunt can be conditional on the signal received. A strategy now consists of a signal to send and an act in the Stag Hunt for each possible signal received. Just as before, signals have no preexisting meaning. Meaning now must co-evolve with behavior in the Stag Hunt.

In the Stag Hunt game, each player has two possible acts: Hunt Stag, Hunt Hare. Payoffs in one canonical Stag Hunt are:

	Stag	Hare
Stag	4,4	0,3
Hare	3,0	3,3

There are two equilibria, one in which both players hunt Stag and one in which they both hunt Hare. The former is better for both players, but each runs a risk by hunting Stag. If the other hunts Hare, the Stag hunter gets nothing. Hare hunters run no such risk. For this reason, conventional evolutionary dynamics favors the Hare hunting equilibrium.

Zollman finds that with interactions with neighbors on a spatial grid and imitate-the-best learning, pre–play signaling evolves such that all players end up hunting Stag. This happens even though the signaling systems are not all the same. We end up with a heterogeneous population that has spontaneously learned both to signal and to use those signals to cooperate. (Grim, Kokalis, Tafti, and Kilb had already used imitation dynamics on a spatial grid in their signaling game with food sources and predators.[16])

The foregoing papers are confined to interactions with neighbors on a special kind of structure—a spatial grid with edges wrapped to

---

[16] Grim et al. 2000; See also the review in Grim et al. 2004.

form a torus. Elliott Wagner extends the analysis to arbitrary inter-action networks.[17] He also considers not only the nice case of two states, signals and acts, states equiprobable, but also our problem cases with unequal probabilities and bigger games.

He finds that the network structure is very important for wheth-er individuals learn to signal, and for whether they learn the same signaling systems or evolve regional dialects. Small world networks are highly conducive to arriving at uniform signaling across the population, and they are remarkably effective in promoting effi-cient signaling even in our problem cases.

Belief learning

Let us move up to the simplest form of belief learning, and see what difference it makes. We now assume that the agents involved know the payoff structure of the game, but do not directly observe what the other player did. What happens with best response dynamics? In general, players *may not know* what a best response is. They know what they did, they know whether or not they got a payoff, and they know the structure of the game. So if they did get a payoff signaling worked, and the best response to the other player's last act is to do the same thing in the same situation. In the special case where each player only has two choices, if they did not get a payoff the best response is clearly to try the other thing.

But in the general case, where there are more than two states, acts, and consequences, plays which lead to no payoff leave the players somewhat in the dark. The receiver knows what she did, and what signal she got, but not which of the states the sender saw. The sender knows what the state was and which signal was sent, but not which of the inappropriate acts was done. Neither knows enough to determine the best response. In such a case, we might consider a weak version of the rule in which she chooses at random

---

[17] Wagner 2009.

between alternatives which might be a best response consistent which what she knows. Call this *best response for all we know*.

The special case of two states, signals and acts is different. If signaling does not succeed, each player can figure out what the other did since the other had only two choices. Best response dynamics here is well defined. How does it do? The following analysis is due to Kevin Zollman.

Pure *best response* dynamics can get trapped in cycles and never learn to signal.[18] Our primitive belief learners are outsmarting each other! Let us try making them a little less eager to be rational. Every once and a while a player best-responds to the other's previous action, but most of the time he just keeps doing the same thing mindlessly. This is *best response with inertia*. You can think of each as flipping her own coin to decide whether to best respond on this round or not. (The coins can be biased.) Acting in accord with best response with inertia, our agents now always learn to signal. With probability one, they sooner or later hit on a signaling system, and then stick with it forever.

What about signaling games with N signals, states and acts? Now the closest our players can come to best response is *best response for all we know*. On getting a payoff, they know that they did a best response to the other's act, so they stick with it. On a failure all they know is that they didn't do a best response, but they don't know which of the other possible actions was the best response—so they choose at random between those alternatives. Already in the case where N=2, that we have already considered, this kind of learning gets trapped in cycles. So, for the general case, we are led to consider *best response for all we know with inertia*. Individuals either just keep doing what they were doing, or—at random times—best respond for all they know. This is an exceedingly modest form of belief learning, but Zollman shows that here (numbers of states, signals and acts are equal), it always learns to signal. It locks on to

---

[18] Try working out the possibilities yourself.

successful pieces of a signaling system when it finds them, and it explores enough to surely find them all.

Now let us think about where all this thinking about belief learning has led. *Best response for all you know with inertia* just comes to this: *Keep doing what you have been doing except once in a while pay attention and if you fail try something different* (at random). So redescribed, this learning rule does not require beliefs or strategic thinking at all! The cognitive resources required are even more modest than those required for reinforcement learning, since one need not keep track of accumulated payoffs—and it always works.

Learning to signal

How hard is it to learn to signal? This depends on our criterion of success for the learning rule. If success means spontaneous generation of signaling in many situations, then all the kinds of learning that we have surveyed pass the test. In particular, all forms of reinforcement learning work, although some work better than others. If it means learning to signal with probability one in all Lewis signaling games, a simple payoff-based learning rule will do the trick. It is easy to learn to signal.

9

Generalizing Signaling Games: Synonyms, Bottlenecks, Category Formation

Generalizing Sender-Receiver

To require that the number of states, acts and signals are equal is a drastic restriction. It may make sense to load up the model with all possible symmetries in order to demonstrate the power of spontaneous symmetry-breaking, but for a naturalistic account of signaling we need to move beyond these very special cases. Some organisms may have a quite limited repertoire of signals, while others—in particular ourselves—may seem to have an embarrassment of riches. So we have cases of too few signals and too many signals.[1] Other mismatches are possible. There may not be enough acts to respond effectively to all the states.

In our simplest model, we also imposed an extreme symmetry on payoffs. If an act was "right" for a state, both sender and receiver got a payoff of one, otherwise a payoff of zero. In general, we should consider all sorts of payoffs in including ones where sender and receiver are in full or partial conflict. We will discuss such cases in a later chapter. Here we maintain the assumption that in all contingencies sender and receiver get the same payoff. But even where sender and receiver continue to have pure common interest, relaxing

---

[1] Wärneryd 1993 considers the case where there are too many signals. Donaldson, Lachmann, and Bergstrom 2007 discuss mismatches in general.

the strict assumptions on payoffs imposed so far may lead to new phenomena.[2]

Many states

If states of the world are whatever the organism can discriminate, then for all but the most perceptually limited organisms there are very many states indeed. Even for organisms with rich signaling systems, such as ourselves, there are more states than will fit comfortably within our signaling systems. The evolution of signals must somehow deal with this fact. We can consider miniature versions by looking at signaling games with more states than signals or acts.

Suppose we have three states, but only two signals and two acts. Let us say that act 1 is the right act for state 1 and act 2 is the right act for state 2. If we ignore state 3, payoffs are just as they would be in a two-state signaling game, but what about state 3?

	Act 1	Act 2
State 1	1, 1	0, 0
State 2	0, 0	1, 1
State 3	?, ?	?, ?

There are various alternatives. It could be that one of these acts is also "right" for state 3. For example, act 1 might be right for state 3. Signaling system equilibria are not yet defined for such games, but there seems to be an obvious candidate. That is one composed of a sender's strategy that maps states 1 and 3 onto the same signal, which elicits act 1 from the receiver, and which maps state 2 onto the other signal, which the receiver's strategy maps to act 2. A realization is shown in figure 9.1:

---

[2] Lewis 1969 allows this, but does not go very far in exploring its consequences.

	Act 1	Act 2
State 1	1, 1	0, 0
State 2	0, 0	1, 1
State 3	1, 1	0, 0

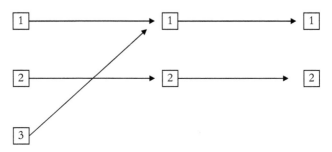

Figure 9.1: A signaling system where there are many states.

These signaling systems are optimal for sender and receiver, and they are evolutionarily stable strategies, just as in the original signaling games. In the equilibrium shown, we could say that signal 1 carries disjunctive information. It indicates "state 1 or state 3." Alternatively, from the point of view of the signaling system, states 1 and 3 are treated as if they were a single state. So, as David Lewis pointed out in *Convention*, we could call states 1 and 3 a single state and assimilate this case to the original 2 state, 2 signal, 2 act model.

At the other extreme, it might be that neither act is any good for state 3. Perhaps state 3 is the proximity of a predator that will get you whether you do act 1 or act 2. The payoffs might look like this:

	Act 1	Act 2
State 1	1, 1	0, 0
State 2	0, 0	1, 1
State 3	0, 0	0, 0

Now there are no evolutionarily stable strategies. The reason is that it doesn't matter what signal is sent in state 3. The only acts available are ineffectual. No matter what natives do in state 3, mutants who do something different in state 3 will do as well as natives. Any equilibrium that does the right thing in states 1 and 2 is as good as it gets.

We looked at two extreme cases, but it is plausible to suppose that many cases are intermediate between the two. Consider:

	Act 1	Act 2
State 1	1, 1	0, 0
State 2	0, 0	1, 1
State 3	a, a	b, b

where a is greater than b. Then a signaling system that uses one signal which elicits act 1 in both states 1 and 3 is evolutionarily stable just as before. It gives the participants the best possible payoff. The intermediate cases look like figure 1. Simulations show reinforcement learners rapidly learning to use such a signaling system.

The example illustrates a general point. In general, where there are many states, a signaling system partitions the states. Evolution of a signaling system is *evolution of a system of categories* used by that system. That evolution is driven by pragmatics—by the available acts and payoffs.

Many signals

Suppose that there is an abundance of signals, relative to the available states and acts. Then if all the signals are used, an efficient system of signals will include functional *synonyms*, which are used in the same states and lead to the same acts. On the other hand, there are efficient equilibria where some signals are never used. As recently shown by Matina Donaldson, Michael Lachmann and

Carl Bergstrom,[3] the concept of evolutionary stability here has no teeth. No equilibrium is evolutionarily stable.

There are, nevertheless, many equilibria where complete information about the state is transmitted, and players always get paid. Consider the simplest case with two states, three signals, and two acts, with one act being right for each state and the states equiprobable. Payoffs are just:

	State 1	State 2
Act 1	1,1	0,0
Act 2	0,0	1,1

Figure 9.2 shows some cases of synonyms:

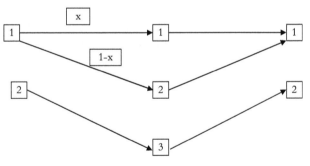

Figure 9.2: Synonyms.

Signals 1 and 2 are used with probability x and (1−x) respectively. They both indicate state 1 and lead to act 1, and so may be regarded as functional synonyms. Every value of x gives one equilibrium, so we have a whole line of equilibria here.

Figure 9.3 shows a signaling equilibrium where synonyms have died out.

---

[3] Donaldson, Lachmann, and Bergstrom 2007. This is the first systematic treatment of the equilibrium structure in these signaling games.

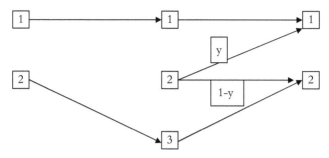

Figure 9.3: No synonyms.

In this equilibrium the sender sends signal 1 exclusively in state 1, signal 3 exclusively in state 2, and never sends signal 2. The receiver may have propensities to respond in signal 2 in various ways, but these are never exercised. Every value of y gives an equilibrium, so we have a whole line of equilibria here.

Now notice that the line of equilibria in figure 2 and the line of equilibria in figure 3 are connected—they share a point. If x = 1 and y =1, we are in both pictures. But now it should be apparent that if y = 0 in figure 3, we have a point that is shared with another line of synonym equilibria—as shown in figure 9.4.

All these equilibria are perfectly good for signaling, and they are all connected in one big component of signaling systems. There is one continuous path through all of them.

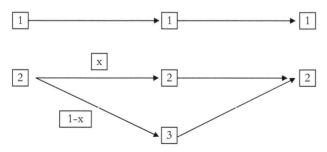

Figure 9.4: More synonyms.

With such a rich set of signaling systems, which will you get? That is a question that cannot be answered by equilibrium analysis, but must be addressed in terms of the dynamics. The answer may depend on the dynamic law, and on the starting point. One possibility would be to use reinforcement learning on acts operating on repeated encounters between a sender and receiver. We start with everything symmetrical—one ball of each color, so to speak, in each sender's and receiver's urn.

One might expect that with this dynamics and this starting point reinforcement would eliminate synonyms. One of the synonyms would be used a little more, get reinforced more, used even more, and take over—so the thought goes.[4] But this verbally plausible argument is incorrect. Synonyms are formed and they persist.

A different dynamics could give quite a different result. In replicator dynamics, our basic model of differential reproduction in a large population, this situation is structurally unstable. Adding a little uniform mutation to the large population model will tend to collapse components to points, and to stabilize synonyms. Finite population models may allow the state to drift around the component of equilibria. A full analysis remains to be done.

Few signals

Some agents may have appropriate acts for the states, but too few signals to coordinate states with acts. This is the case of an informational bottleneck. Informational bottlenecks affect humans as well as other organisms because, although we have a rich repertoire of signals, we may not have the time or means to utilize it in a specific situation.

---

[4] The thought is based on a misconception. Once the players have learned to treat two signals as synonyms, the relative reinforcement between them is a Pólya urn process. Then the synonyms may end up being used with any kind of relative frequency. This is what we see in the simulations.

Signaling games with information bottlenecks present quite a different picture. Bottlenecks can create suboptimal evolutionarily stable strategies, as shown by the following example of Matina Donaldson, Michael Lachmann, and Carl Bergstrom.

	Act 1	Act 2	Act 3
State 1	7, 7	0, 0	2, 2
State 2	4, 4	6, 6	0, 0
State 3	0, 0	5, 5	10, 10

We suppose that the states are equiprobable. If there were three signals, then agents could always behave optimally, for an average payoff of 7 ⅔. But there are only two signals. Then they might settle into the signaling system shown in figure 9.5.

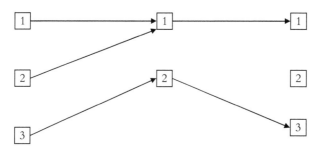

Figure 9.5: An efficient solution to a bottleneck.

This is an evolutionarily stable strategy. It is not a bad way of dealing with the informational bottleneck, with an average payoff of 7.

But this is not the only evolutionarily stable strategy. Another is shown in figure 9.6.

This equilibrium is suboptimal, with an average payoff of 6. But it is still a strict equilibrium of the two-person game, and an

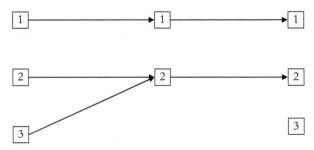

Figure 9.6: An inefficient solution to the same bottleneck.

evolutionarily stable strategy.[5] A reasonable adaptive dynamics can fall into this state.

These two equilibria represent two different ways in which a signaling system can categorize the world. But, unlike the examples of the first section of this chapter, we see that the system of categories that evolves may not be optimal.

Systems of categories

In a given signaling game, we have seen how the signals evolve so as to embody a system of categories. States that the sender maps onto the same signal belong to the same category according to the signaling system. But signals may be used in different situations. They may become "decoupled" from a particular signaling game, at least in the quite rigid sense which we have given to signaling games.[6] How should we think about this process?

We can move part of the way to an answer by broadening our model of a signaling game. Suppose the sender sometimes is in a position to observe the state exactly, but sometimes can only determine the member of some coarser system of categories. For example, suppose that sometimes a monkey may be able to

---

[5] In both one and two population settings.
[6] Compare Sterelny 2003 on decoupled representations.

determine whether a leopard, eagle, or snake is present; sometimes only whether there is an aerial or terrestrial predator. We can incorporate this in our model by letting nature not only choose a state, but also choose an observational partition. Sometimes nature may choose the finest partition whose members are the states themselves, sometimes a coarser partition. The sender sees only the member of the partition in which the true state resides. A sender's strategy now maps members of observational partitions to signals.

There may be acts optimal for some coarse-grained information that are different from the acts optimal for any specific state. We can put them in the model as well. Then it is quite possible to evolve a signaling system where some signals represent disjunctions of states.[7] More generally, we can evolve a signaling system that incorporates a system of categories of different specificity.

Consider a game with three equiprobable states. There are three acts, one right for each state, just as in the simplest signaling game:

	Act 1	Act 2	Act 3
State 1	1,1	0,0	0,0
State 2	0,0	1,1	0,0
State 3	0,0	0,0	1,1

but there are also three other acts that are less than optimal in each state, but also less risky:

	Act 1	Act 2	Act 3	Act 4	Act 5	Act 6
State 1	1,1	0,0	0,0	.6,.6	0,0	.8,.8
State 2	0,0	1,1	0,0	.6,.6	.8,.8	0,0
State 3	0,0	0,0	1,1	0,0	.8,.8	.8,.8

---

[7] I first floated this idea in a discussion of the evolution of logical inference in Skyrms 2000.

Using the fact that states are equiprobable, we get the average payoff for sets of states:

	Act 1	Act 2	Act 3	Act 4	Act 5	Act 6
State 1	1,1	0,0	0,0	.6,.6	0,0	.8,.8
State 2	0,0	1,1	0,0	.6,.6	.8,.8	0,0
State 3	0,0	0,0	1,1	0,0	.8,.8	.8,.8
1 or 2	.5,.5	.5,.5	0,0	.6,.6	.4,.4	.4,.4
2 or 3	0,0	.5,.5	.5,.5	.3,.3	.8,.8	.4,.4
1 or 3	.5,.5	0,0	.5,.5	.3,.3	.4,.4	.8,.8

A sender's strategy in this extended game maps sender's observational states to signals sent, and a signaling system equilibrium is an equilibrium that gives optimal payoffs to the players. For instance:

State 1 => Signal 1 => Act 1
State 2 => Signal 2 => Act 2
State 3 => Signal 3 => Act 3
S1 or S2 => Signal 4 => Act 4
S2 or S3 => Signal 5 => Act 5
S1 or S3 => Signal 6 => Act 6

This is evolutionarily stable in our extended signaling game.[8] Signals 4, 5, and 6 might be thought of as having a proto-truth-functional content relative to signals 1, 2, and 3.

Consider the alternative observational partitions of states implicit in this little example. There is the finest partition, where the observer sees the state exactly. There are three coarsenings of this partition, {S1-or-S2, not-(S1-or-S2)}, {S2-or-S3, not-(S2-or-S3)}, {S1-or-S3, not-(S1-or-S3)}. It should be obvious how to construct more complex examples. We have an account of the evolution of systems of categories. It can happen without any

---

[8] There is no guarantee that this will always happen.

complex rational thought, simply as a consequence of the action of adaptive dynamics.

Conclusion

Once we allow modest generalizations of signaling games, interesting new phenomena appear. We have synonyms and bottlenecks. We have the pragmatics of signaling inducing systems of categories into which states are sorted. These new phenomena raise new questions. Do synonyms persist or do they fade away? Are bottlenecks permanent or is there a plausible account of how adaptive dynamics can eliminate them? How can agents combine the information from various levels of categories? We have seen that for at least one plausible dynamics synonyms persist. We will try to shed a little light on the two remaining questions in subsequent chapters.

10

Inventing New Signals[1]

New signals?

Agents may not have enough signals to convey the information that they need to communicate. Why can't the agents simply invent new signals to remedy the situation? We would like to have a simple, easily studied model of this process. That is to say, we want to move beyond the closed models that we have studied so far, where the theorist fixes the signals, to an open model in which the space of signals itself can evolve. I can find no such account in the literature. I would like to suggest one here.

Invention in nature: genetic evolution

The fixed number of signals in a Lewis signaling game is, after all, an artificial limitation. In nature those signals had to be invented. If they were invented, new signals could be invented as well. The range of potential new signals is highly dependent on the nature of the signalers. The availability of new signals for bacteria, for instance, is constrained by molecular biology. Even so, over evolutionary time, different species of gram–negative bacteria[2] have managed to

---

[1] For more analysis of this model of inventing new signals, see Skyrms and Zabell forthcoming.

[2] So called, because they do not take up the violet stain in Gram's test. Gram negative bacteria tend to be pathogens.

invent different quorum-sensing signaling systems by evolving ways to make small side-chain modifications to a basic signaling molecule.[3]

Quorum-sensing was discovered in bacterium, *Vibrio fisheri* that inhabits the light organ of the Hawaiian squid, *Euprymna scolopes*. *Euprymna* is a nocturnal hunter. If there is a full moon, it can be highly visible against the illuminated surface of the water and become prey itself. It uses its light organ to counter this and render itself less conspicuous to its predators. The light, itself, is made by the bacteria living in the light organ. The squid supplies the bacteria with nutrients and the bacteria provide the squid with camouflage.

The bacteria regulate light production by quorum-sensing. They produce a small, diffusible (AHL) signaling molecule. It is auto-inducing—when its concentration in the ambient environment increases, the bacteria produce more of it. This happens inside the light organ. High enough concentrations, a *quorum*, trigger gene expression that turns on the light. (The squid turns the lights off by simply expelling bacteria from the organ and replacing them with seawater.)

Subsequently, quorum-sensing signaling based on slight modification of the AHL molecule has been found in other gram negative bacteria. *Psuedomonas aeruginosa* uses quorum-sensing to turn on virulence and biofilm formation in the lungs of cystic fibrosis patients. A bacterium (*Erwinia carotovora*)[4] that rots plants uses AHL-based quorum-sensing to turn on both virulence against the plant and production of antibiotics against competitor bacteria that could also exploit the damaged host. An ancestral signaling system has been modified for a variety of different uses.

Gram positive bacteria[5]—including such sometimes nasty customers as *Staphylococcus aureus*—have parallel signaling systems based on different signaling molecules. In a review of quorum-sensing, Melissa Miller and Bonnie Bassler conclude:

---

[3] Taga and Bassler 2003; Miller and Bassler 2001.

[4] See Miller and Bassler 2001.

[5] So called, because they do take up the dye in Gram's stain test.

Bacteria occupying diverse niches have broadly adapted quorum sensing systems to optimize them for regulating a variety of activities. In every case quorum sensing confers on bacteria the ability to communicate and to alter behavior in response to the presence of other bacteria. Quorum sensing allows a population of individuals to coordinate global behavior and thus act as a multi-cellular unit. Although the study of quorum sensing is only at its beginning, we are now in a position to gain fundamental insight into how bacteria build community networks.[6]

Evolution creates and modifies signals in even the most primitive organisms.

Invention in nature: cultural evolution

Invention in genetic evolution may be highly constrained and take a long time. In cultural evolution and in individual learning there is more latitude for new signals, and evolution of the signaling space is ongoing.

For instance, the vocal capabilities of monkeys allow for a range of potential signals that, when required, can be tapped by learning. Vervet monkeys who have encountered a new predator have learned both a new signal and a new evasive action:

Vervets on the Cameroon savanna are sometimes attacked by feral dogs. When they see a dog, they respond much as Amboseli vervets respond to a leopard; they give loud alarm calls and run into trees. Elsewhere in the Cameroon, however, vervets live in forests where they are hunted by armed humans who track them down with the aid of dogs. In these circumstances, where loud alarm calls and conspicuous flight into trees would only increase the monkeys' likelihood of being shot, the vervets' alarm calls to dogs are short, quiet and cause others to flee silently into dense bushes where humans cannot follow.[7]

---

[6] Miller and Bassler 2001.
[7] Cheney and Seyfarth 1990, 169 who refer to Kavanaugh 1980.

The dynamics of learning, when the need arises, is able to modify the signaling system in a highly efficient way.

General principles

There is nothing really mysterious about the modification of the vervets' signaling system described above. First, nature presents the monkeys with a new state—one different from "all clear" or from the presence of any of the familiar predators. The salience of this new state, "dogs and hunters," is established when the first monkey is shot. An appropriate new escape action is discovered. In principle it might be discovered just by group trial and error, although we do not want to sell the vervets short on cognitive ability.

Once we have the new state and the appropriate new action we are in the kind of information bottleneck that we described in Chapter 1. We have seen that such bottlenecks can sometimes spontaneously arise from dynamics of evolution and learning. What is required is the invention of a new signal. Senders have lots of potential signals available to them. These are just actions—in this case, vocalizations—that receivers are liable to notice. Senders try potential signals, receivers try actions, and happy coincidences are rewarded.

General principles of invention emerge. We can suppose that there are acts that the sender can take which the receiver will notice. These could be tried out as signals—either on a short time scale or a very long one. The potential signals may be sounds, or movements, or secretions of some chemical. They may bear some resemblance to other signals, or to other features of the environment that receivers already tend to monitor. With some probability a new signal can be actualized—a sender will send it and a receiver will pay attention to it.

Verbal statement of general principles is not hard, but we still lack a simple model that can serve as a focal point for analysis. How should we incorporate the invention of new signals in the Lewis model of signaling games? We would like to retain as much as possible the simplicity and analytical tractability of the original model, while having an open rather than a closed set of signals.

The Chinese restaurant process

We begin with an example that may appear overly fanciful, but which will nevertheless turn out to be relevant. Imagine a Chinese restaurant, with an infinite number of tables, each of which can hold an infinite number of guests. People enter one at a time and sit down according to the following rule. If N guests are already seated, the next guest sits to the left of each of the N guests already seated with probability $1/(N+1)$, and goes to an unoccupied table with probability $1/(N + 1)$. [One could imagine a ghost sitting at the first unoccupied table, and then the rule would be to sit to the left of someone—including the phantom guest—with equal probability.][8]

The first person to enter sits at the first unoccupied table, since no one but the phantom guest is there. The phantom guest moves to the first unoccupied table. The second person to enter now has equal probability of sitting with the first, or at an unoccupied table. Should the second join the first, the third has a $2/3$ chance of sitting at their table and a $1/3$ chance of starting a new one. Should the second start a new table, the phantom guest moves on, and the third will join one or the other or start a third table with equal probability. This is the *Chinese restaurant process*, which has a surprising number of applications, and which has been well studied as a problem in abstract probability theory.[9]

Since there is only one phantom, the probability of a new table being selected goes down as the number of guests goes up. But if there is an infinite stream of guests, at any point in the process the

---

[8] Variations place some number of phantom guests at the first unoccupied table.

[9] Aldous 1985; Pitman 1995.

probability that no new table will ever be selected is always zero. In the limit an infinite number of tables will be occupied. Nevertheless, for long finite stretches of time the number of occupied tables may be small.

To get a feel for the process, suppose that four guests have entered. We could have four tables occupied (1+1+1+1), or three (2+1+1) or two {(2+2) or (3+1)} or one (4). The last possibility, that all guests sit at the first table is six times as probable as the first alternative in which each guest chooses a different table.[10] The possibility of three guests at one table and one at the other can be realized in four different ways. Numbering the guests in order of appearance, they are: {1,2,3}{4}, {2,3,4}{1}, {1,3,4} {2}, and {1,2,4}{3}. Each has equal probability—which guests are at which tables does not matter.

Adding up the probabilities of the ways of getting the (3+1) pattern we get (8/24). Likewise, we find the probability of the (2+2) pattern as (3/24). The probability that two tables are occupied is the sum of these, or (11/24). We may notice in passing that the probability of unequal occupation of two tables (3+1) is much more likely than that of equal occupation (2+2). The probabilities of different numbers of tables being occupied are:

One Table:	(6/24)
Two Tables:	(11/24)
Three Tables:	(6/24)
Four Tables:	(1/24)

As more and more guests come in, the expected number of occupied tables grows as the logarithm of the number of guests.

[10] $(1)(1/2)(2/3)(3/4) = (6/24)$ vs. $(1)(1/2)(1/3)(1/4) = (1/24)$.

Hoppe's urn

If we neglect the seating order of guests at a table, and just keep track of the number of guests at each table, the process is equivalent to a simple urn model. In 1984 Hoppe introduced what he called "Pólya-like urns" in connection with "neutral" evolution—evolution in the absence of selection pressure. In a classical Pólya urn process, we start with an urn containing various colored balls. Then we proceed as follows: A ball is drawn at random. It is returned to the urn with another ball of the same color. All colors are treated in exactly the same way. We can recognize the Pólya urn process as a special case of reinforcement learning in which there is no distinction worth learning—all choices (colors) are reinforced equally. The probabilities in a Pólya urn process converge to a random limit. They are guaranteed to converge to something, but that something can be anything.

To the Pólya urn, Hoppe adds a black ball—the *mutator*.[11] The mutator does not mutate in the sense explored in earlier chapters, where colors in the urn mutate to one another. Rather, it brings new colors into the game. If the black ball is drawn, it is returned to the urn and a ball of an entirely new color is added to the urn. (There are, of course, lots of variations possible. There might be more than one black ball initially, and Hoppe considered this possibility. The number of black balls might not be fixed, but might itself evolve in various ways. Here, however, we will stick to the simplest case.) The Hoppe-Pólya urn model was meant as a model for neutral selection, where there are a vast number of potential mutations which convey no selective advantage.

(It also has an alternative life in the Bayesian theory of induction, having essentially been invented in 1838 by the logician Augustus de Morgan to deal with the prediction of the emergence of novel categories.)[12]

---

[11] Hoppe 1984.
[12] I owe my knowledge of this to Sandy Zabell. For both history and analytical discussion see Zabell 1992, 2005.

It is evident that the Hoppe-Pólya urn process and the Chinese restaurant process are the same thing. Hoppe's colors correspond to the tables in the Chinese restaurant; the mutator ball corresponds to the phantom guest. After a finite number, N, of iterations the N guests in the restaurant, or the N balls in Hoppe's urn, are partitioned into some number of categories. The categories are colors for the urn, tables for the restaurant. But the partitions we end up with can be different each time; they depend on the luck of the draw. We have *random partitions*, which may have a different number of categories, different numbers of individuals in each category, and different individuals filling out the numbers—all of which we have seen in our little example with four guests.

We also saw in our example that all ways of realizing the pattern of one table with three guests and one table with one were equally likely. This is generally true of the process. All that affects the probability is a specification of the number of tables that have a given number of guests. This specification is called the partition vector. In our example is it 1 table with one guest, 0 tables with 2 guests, 1 table with 3 guests, 0 tales with four guests: $<1,0,1,0>$? The fact that any arrangement of guests with the same partition vector has the same probability is called *partition exchangeability*, and it is the key to mathematical analysis of the process.

There are explicit formulas to calculate probabilities and expectations of classes of outcomes after a finite number of trials. The expected number of categories—of colors of ball in Hoppe's urn or the expected number of tables in the Chinese restaurant—will be of particular interest to us, because the number of colors in a sender's urn will correspond to the number of signals in use. This is given by a very simple formula.[13] Results are plotted in figure 10.1:

---

[13] SUM (from i=0 to i=N-1) $1/(1+i)$.

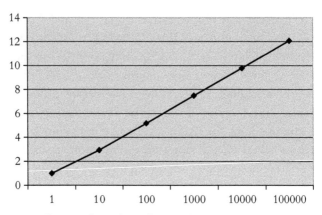

Figure 10.1: Expected number of categories.

For even quite large numbers of trials, the expected number of categories is quite modest. There is something else that I would like to emphasize. For a given number of categories, the distribution of trials among those categories is not uniform. We can illustrate this with an example that is simple enough to graph. Suppose we have ten trials and the number of categories turns out to be two (two colors of ball, two tables in the restaurant) which will happen about 28% of the time. This can be realized in five different ways of partitioning 10: $5 + 5, 4 + 6, 3 + 7, 2 + 8, 1 + 9$. There is a simple way of calculating the probability of each—the Ewens sampling formula. The results are graphed in figure 10.2.

The more unequal a division is between the categories, the more likely it is to occur. Some colors are numerous, some are rare. Some tables are much fuller than others. Finally, let us notice that the Hoppe urn can be redescribed in a suggestive way. You can think of it as a way of moving between Pólya urns. The mutator process is kept track of on the side, say with an urn of one black and many white balls. Pick a white ball from the auxiliary urn and you add another white ball, and sample from your current Pólya urn. Pick the black ball from the auxiliary urn and you move to a different Pólya urn with all the old balls and with one more ball of one more

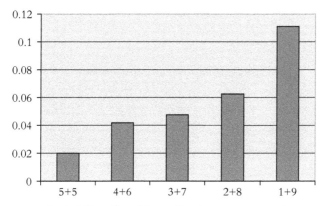

Figure 10.2: Probability of partitions of 10 into two categories.

color. This is a little like moving between games, and we will make it the basis of doing just that.

Reinforcement with invention

We remarked that Pólya urn process can be thought of as reinforcement learning when there is no distinction worth learning—all choices (colors) are reinforced equally. The Hoppe-Pólya urn, then, is a model that adds useless invention to useless learning. That was its original motivation, where different alleles confer no selective advantage.

If we modify the Pólya urn by adding differential reinforcement—where choices are reinforced according to different payoffs—we get the Herrnstein–Roth–Erev model of reinforcement learning of the foregoing chapters. If we modify the Hoppe-Pólya model by adding differential reinforcement, we can get reinforcement learning that is capable of invention.[14]

---

[14] Alternatively, we can interpret this as a model of evolution in a finite, growing population.

Pólya Urn		Hoppe-Pólya Urn
is to	*as*	*is to*
Reinforcement Learning		Reinforcement with Invention

Figure 10.3: Urn models.

Inventing new signals[15]

We use the Hoppe-Pólya urn as a basis for a model of inventing new signals in signaling games. For each state of the world, the sender has an additional choice: *send a new signal*. A new signal is always available. The sender can either send one of the existing signals or send a new one. Receivers always pay attention to a new signal. (A new signal means new signal that is noticed, failures being taken account of by making the probability of a successful new signal smaller.) Receivers, when confronted with a new signal, just act at random. We equip them with equal initial propensities for the acts.

Now we need to specify exactly how learning proceeds. Nature chooses a state and the sender either chooses a new signal, or one of the old signals. If there is no new signal the model works just as before. If a new signal is introduced, it either leads to a successful action or not. When there is no success, the system returns to the state it was in before the experiment with a new signal was tried.

---

[15] We note that the same kind of urn model could be used for inventing new actions on the part of the receiver. But if this were done, we would need to specify the payoffs of potential new actions in each state. There is no general principled way to do this, although in specific applications there might be some plausible approach.

But if the new signal leads to a successful action, both sender and receiver are reinforced. The reinforcement now constitutes the sender's new initial propensity to send the signal in the state in which it was just sent. The receiver now begins keeping track of the success of acts taken upon receiving the new signal. In terms of the urn model, the receiver activates an urn for the signal, with one ball for each possible act, and adds to that urn the reinforcement for the successful act just taken. The sender now considers the new signal not only in the states in which it was tried out, but also considers it a possibility in other states. So, in terms of the urn model, a ball for the new signal is added to each sender's urn, in addition to the reinforcement ball added to the urn for the state that has just occurred.[16] The new signal has now established itself. We have

Before Successful Invention

Sender Urn 1: R, G, B	Receiver Urn R: A1, A2
Sender Urn 2: R, G, B	Receiver Urn G: A1, A2

After Successful Invention
(in State 2 with Act 2)

	Receiver Urn R: A1, A2
Sender Urn 1: R, G, B, Y	
	Receiver Urn G: A1, A2
Sender Urn 2: R, G, B, Y, Y	
	Receiver Urn Y: A1, A2, A2

Figure 10.4: In state 2 a black ball is drawn, act 2 is tried and is successful. A yellow ball is added to both senders' urns and a reinforcement yellow ball is added to the urn for state 2. The receiver adds an urn for the signal yellow, and adds an extra ball to that urn for act 2.

[16] We could add a fractional ball, and make fraction a parameter to adjust the strength of the sender's generalization of the new signal from one situation to another. Here we just stick to the simplest formulation where strength of generalization is one.

moved from a Lewis signaling game with N signals to one with N+1 signals.

In summary, one of three things can happen:

1. No new signal tried, and the game is unchanged. Reinforcement proceeds as in a game with a fixed number of signals.

2. A new signal is tried but without success, and the game is unchanged.

3. A new signal is tried with success, and the game changes from one with n states, m signals and o acts to one with n states, m+1 signals, o acts.

Starting with nothing

If we can invent new signals, we can start with no signals at all, and see how the process evolves. Consider the three-state, three-act Lewis signaling game with states equiprobable. As before, exactly one act is right for each state. We can gain some insight into this

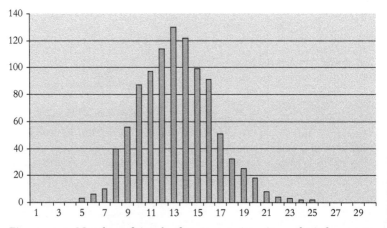

Figure 10.5: Number of signals after 100,000 iterations of reinforcement with invention. Frequency in 1,000 trials.

complicated process from our understanding of the Hoppe urn. In fact, once senders learn to signal successfully in a given state, the sender's urn for that state is a Hoppe urn.

If we ran the process forever, we would end up with an infinite number of signals. But if we run a large finite number of iterations, we would expect a not-so-large number of signals. In simulations of our model of invention, starting with no signals at all, the number of signals after 100,000 iterations ranged from 5 to 25. (A histogram of the final number of signals in 1,000 trials is shown in figure 10.5.)

Avoiding pooling traps

Recall that in a version of this game with the number of signals fixed at 3, classical reinforcement learning sometimes falls into a partial pooling equilibrium. In basic Roth–Erev reinforcement learning with initial propensities of 1, about 9% of the trials led to imperfect information transmission. Using reinforcement with invention, starting with no signals, 1,000 trials *all* ended up with efficient signaling. Signalers went beyond inventing the three requisite signals. Lots of synonyms were created. By inventing more signals, they avoided the traps of partial pooling equilibria.

And recall that in the game with two states, two acts, and the number of signals fixed at 2, if the states had unequal probabilities agents sometimes fell into a total pooling equilibrium—in which no information at all is transmitted. In such an equilibrium the receiver would simply do the act suited for the most probable state and ignore the signal and the sender would send signals with probabilities that were not sensitive to the state. The probability of falling into total pooling increased as the disparity in probabilities became greater. When one state has probability .6, failure of information transfer hardly ever happens. At probability .7 it happens 5% of the time. This number rises to 22% for probability .8, and 44%

for probability .9. Highly unequal state probabilities appear to be a major obstacle to the evolution of efficient signaling.

If we take the extreme case in which one state has probability .9, start with no signals at all, and let the players invent signals as above they reliably learn to signal. In 1,000 trials they never fell into a pooling trap; they always learned a signaling system. They invented their way out of the trap. The invention of new signals makes efficient signaling a much more robust phenomenon.

Synonyms

Let us look at our results a little more closely. Typically we get efficient signaling with lots of synonyms. How much work are the synonyms doing? Consider the following trial of three-state, three-act signaling game, starting with no signals and proceeding with 100,000 iterations of learning with invention.

Trail 2:

signal 1 probabilities in states 0,1,2	0.00006, **0.71670**, 0.00006
signal 2 probabilities in states 0,1,2	0.00006, **0.28192**, 0.00006
signal 3 probabilities in states 0,1,2	0.09661, 0.00006, 0.00080
signal 4 probabilities in states 0,1,2	0.00946, 0.00042, 0.00012
signal 5 probabilities in states 0,1,2	**0.86867**, 0.00012, 0.00006
signal 6 probabilities in states 0,1,2	0.00006, 0.00006, **0.81005**
signal 7 probabilities in states 0,1,2	0.02393, 0.00006, 0.00012
signal 8 probabilities in states 0,1,2	0.00006, 0.00006, **0.14338**
signal 9 probabilities in states 0,1,2	0.00006, 0.00018, 0.04449
signal 10 probabilities in states 0,1,2	0.00012, 0.00006, 0.00043
signal 11 probabilities in states 0,1,2	0.00012, 0.00012, 0.00006
signal 12 probabilities in states 0,1,2	0.00054, 0.00012, 0.00018
signal 13 probabilities in states 0,1,2	0.00018, 0.00006, 0.00012

Notice that a few of the signals (shown in boldface) are doing most of the work. In state 1, signal 5 is sent 87% of the time. Signals 1 and 2 function as significant synonyms for state 2, being sent more than 99.5% of the time. Signals 6 and 8 are the major synonyms for state 3. The pattern is fairly typical. Very often, many of the signals that have been invented end up little used. This is just what we should expect from what we know about the Hoppe urn. Even without any selective advantage, the distribution of reinforcements among categories tends to be highly unequal, as was shown in figure 10.2. Might not infrequently used signals simply fall out of use entirely?

Noisy forgetting

Nature forgets things by having individuals die. Some strategies (phenotypes) simply go extinct. This cannot really happen in the replicator dynamics—an idealization where unsuccessful types get rarer and rarer but never actually vanish. And it cannot happen in Roth–Erev reinforcement where unsuccessful acts are dealt with in much the same way.

Evolution in a finite population is different. In the models of Sebastian Shreiber,[17] a finite population of different phenotypes is modeled as an urn of balls of different colors. Successful reproduction of a phenotype corresponds to the addition of balls of the same color. So far this is identical to the basic model of reinforcement learning. But individuals also die. We transpose the idea to learning dynamics to get a model of reinforcement learning with noisy forgetting.

For individual learning, this model may be more realistic than the usual model of geometrical discounting. That model, which discounts the past by keeping some fixed fraction of each ball at each update, may be best suited for aggregate learning—where individual fluctuations are averaged out. But individual learning is

---

[17] Shreiber 2001.

noisy, and it may be worth looking at an urn model of individual reinforcement with noisy forgetting.

Inventing and forgetting signals

We put together these ideas to get learning with invention and with noisy forgetting, and apply it to signaling. It is just like the model of inventing new signals except for the random dying-out of old reinforcement, implemented by random removal of balls from the sender's urns.

The idea may be implemented in various ways. Nature might, with some probability, pick an urn at random, pick a ball from it at random and throw it away. (The probability is the forgetting rate.) Or alternatively, Jason McKenzie Alexander suggests that nature pick an urn at random, pick a color in that urn at random, and throw a ball of that color away. Either way, there is one less ball in that urn and the trial is over.

Now, it is possible that the number of balls of one color, or even balls of all colors could hit zero in a sender's urn. Should we allow this to happen, as long as the color (the signal) is represented in other urns for other states? There is another choice to be made here. If the number of balls of a certain color is zero in all sender's urns, then the corresponding signal is extinct and the receiver's urn corresponding to that signal dies out.

There is a lot of territory to explore in these forgetting models. Preliminary simulations suggest the following. The first kind of forgetting that we took from finite population evolution (balls removed with equal probability) doesn't change the distribution of signals much at all. Usage of synonyms continues to follow a kind of power law distribution, with little-used signals persisting. This makes sense, because mostly it is the frequently used signals that are dying. But Alexander's kind of forgetting can be remarkably effective in pruning little-used signals without disrupting the evolution of efficient signaling. Often, in long simulation runs, we get close to the minimum number of signals needed for an efficient signaling system.

Inventing new signals

We now have a simple, tractable model for the invention of new signals. It can be easily studied by simulation, and connections with well-studied processes from population genetics suggest that analytic results are not completely out of reach. It invites all sorts of interesting variations. Even the most basic model has interesting properties, both by itself and in combination with forgetting.

11

Networks I: Logic and Information Processing

Logic

David Lewis wrote *Convention* in order to use game theory to answer the skeptical doubts about the conventionality of meaning raised by the great American philosopher Willard van Orman Quine. Quine's skepticism was directed at the logical positivists' conventional theory of meaning in the service of a conventional theory of logic. According to the logical positivists, logical truths were true and logical arguments valid by virtue of the meanings of the terms involved.

Quine argued that positivist accounts of convention (by explicit or implicit definition) required the pre-existence of logic. Lewis replied that the existence of a convention can be thought of in a different way, as a strong kind of equilibrium or near-equilibrium in a signaling game played by a population. Lewis did not himself supply an account of how a population might get to signaling-system equilibrium, but we have seen how to do so.

This leaves the question of whether the account thus established in any way supports the doctrine of the conventionality of logic, whose refutation was Quine's ultimate goal. In so far as one's view of logic is expansive—some positivists viewed all of mathematics as logic—the project may seem Quixotic. We begin with the more modest goal of seeing whether we can get *some* logic out of information transfer in sender-receiver games.

I advanced some tentative suggestions in previous work.[1] These involve modifications to the basic Lewis signaling setup. First, the sender may not observe the state of the world exactly. Her observation may rule out some possibilities while leaving a class of others viable. For example, a vervet monkey may detect the presence of a ground predator—leopard or snake—without being able to see which it is. If this happens often enough and if, as is quite possible, the receiver's optimal action given this information is different from both the optimal action for a leopard or for a snake, it is plausible that a special signal could evolve for this sender's information state in exactly the same way as in the original signaling games. I call such a signal *proto truth-functional* because one way of giving its meaning is by the truth function "leopard or snake"—even though the signal itself is just a one-word sentence. Let us postulate a rich signaling environment in which lots of proto-truth functional signals have evolved.

The second modification is to consider multiple senders, each in possession of a different piece of relevant information. For example, suppose one sender on the ground—seeing a movement of grass—sends the proto-truth function "leopard or snake," and another sender, from the vantage point of a tree, sends the proto-truth function "no leopard." (Negative signals that cancel part of an alarm call are not unknown in animal signaling, as we saw in Chapter 2.) Selection favors the receiver who takes the evasive action appropriate for a snake. Such a receiver has performed—or acts as if she has performed—logical inference.

This story was put forward in a tentative and preliminary spirit, and it leaves several important questions hanging. The proto-truth functions were assumed to have already evolved. Could they co-evolve with logical inference, or are they required to exist already? Where are the precise models? Where is their analysis in terms of evolutionary or learning dynamics? We are now in a position to address these questions, and to generalize the account.

---

[1] Skyrms 2000, 2004.

Information processing

It is best to think of our two–sender, one–receiver model as an especially simple case of a problem of *information processing*. Multiple senders send signals that convey different pieces of information and the receiver can benefit from integrating this information. Let us consider some simple examples.

1. Inventing the Code:

Suppose that there are four equiprobable states of nature, and that two individuals are situated to make incomplete observations of the state. The first sees whether it is in {S1, S2} or in {S3, S4} and the second sees whether it is in {S1, S3} or in {S2, S4}. Together they have enough information to pin down the state of nature, but separately they do not. Each sends one of two signals to a receiver who must choose one of four acts. The payoffs favor cooperation. Exactly one act is "right" for each of the states in that each of the individuals is reinforced just in case the "right" act for the state is chosen.

I will not assume here, as I did in the story at the beginning of this chapter, that a convention has already been established for the signals used by the senders. We will make things a little harder and *require that the content of the signals evolve together with the inference*. You could think of sender 1 as waving either a red or a green flag and sender 2 as waving either a yellow or a blue one.[2]

A *signaling system* in this extended Lewis signaling game is a combination of strategies of the three players, two senders and one receiver, such that the receiver always does the right thing for the state. If we run simulations of reinforcement learning, starting with everyone out acting at random, the three individuals typically fall rapidly into one of the possible signaling systems.

---

[2] The receiver will have to be able to differentiate information from the two senders, since they are placed to make different observations.

Consider the flow of information in these signaling systems. Each sender's signal conveys perfect information about her observation—about the partition of states of the world that she can see. The combination of signals has perfect information about the states of the world. Exactly one state corresponds to each combination of signals. And the receiver puts the signals together. The receiver's acts contain perfect information about the state of the world.

2. Inventing the Categories and the Code:

In the foregoing example, we postulated the categories that the senders can observe and thus those that could be embodied in their signals. For example, sender 1 can at best convey the information that the world is in one of the first two states or that it is not. That is all that she can see. In a remarkable analysis, Jeffrey Barrett considers a model where the two senders and one receiver need to interact to spontaneously invent both the categories and the code in order to achieve a signaling system.[3]

In Barrett's game there are four states and four acts, just as before, but each sender can observe exactly the true state of the world. Although each sender now has perfect information, each has only two signals available. There are two information bottlenecks. To achieve a signaling system our three individuals face a daunting task. Senders need to attach their signals to categories in such a way that these categories complement each other and jointly determine the state of the world. The receiver needs to extract the information from these signals. Receivers need to learn at the same time that senders are learning how to categorize, and senders need to learn their complementary categorizations while receivers are learning to extract information from the combination of signals received.

In a signaling system, sender 1 might send her first signal in states 1 and 2 and her second signal otherwise, and sender 2 might send her first signal in states 1 and 3 and her second otherwise. (These are just the categories imposed by observational restrictions in

---

[3] Barrett 2007a, 2007b.

example 1.) But alternatively sender 1 might lump states 1 and 4 together for one signal and states 2 and 3 for another which, together with the same receiver's strategy, would let the combination of signals peg the state of the world.

To my considerable surprise, Barrett found that Roth–Erev reinforcement learners reliably learned to optimally categorize and signal. The categories formed depended on the vicissitudes of chance— sometimes one set, sometimes another—but they always complemented one another in a way that allowed the receiver to do the right thing. Consider the flow of information in the signaling-system equilibria in Barrett's game. Sender's signals do not convey perfect information about their observations, but only partial information. Nevertheless, the combination of signals has perfect information about the states of the world. Exactly one state corresponds to each combination of signals. And the receiver puts the signals together. The receiver's acts contain perfect information about the state of the world.

Senders have learned to cooperate so as to jointly send the maximal information. The receiver has learned to interpret the signals. She has also, in a way, learned to perform a most basic logical inference: from premises p, q to infer the conjunction $p \& q$.

3. Extracting Relevant Information

Appropriate information processing depends on the character of the payoffs. Let us revisit example 1. The two senders again have their categories fixed by observation. Sender 1 can see whether the world is in one of the first two states or not; sender 2 can see whether the state is odd numbered or even numbered. We modify the example so that there are only two relevant acts with the following payoffs:

	Act 1	Act 2
State 1	0	1
State 2	1	0
State 3	1	0
State 4	0	1

Optimal signaling requires the receiver to do act 1 in states 2 and 3 and act 2 otherwise. Although there are only two acts now, the receiver cannot rely on only one sender, since neither has sufficient information. The senders have information about their own categories—their own partitions of the states of the world—but the receiver needs information about a different partition. Reinforcement learners, starting with random exploration, learn optimal signaling here just as well and just as quickly as in the previous examples.

Given optimal signaling, where players are always reinforced, each sender's signal here carries perfect information about her observation and the combination of signals singles out the state of the world. But the receiver's *act* contains only partial information about the state. It is "only as informative as is required" by the pragmatic considerations embodied in the reinforcement structure. The receiver has learned to extract the information that is relevant and to ignore that which is irrelevant.

This operation of filtering out the irrelevant and keeping the relevant is one of the fundamental operations of information processing. Our sensory systems receive an enormous amount of information, only a small fraction of which is passed on to the brain. Our olfactory system, for instance, contains receptors exquisitely tuned to respond to individual molecules. This information is filtered and integrated so that only relevant information makes it to the central processing unit.

We can also see our little example from different perspectives. From the viewpoint of truth-functional logic, the receiver has had to learn how to compute the truth-value of the exclusive disjunction, "*xor*", from the truth values of its constituents. Sender 1 observes whether p is true; sender 2 observes whether q is true. The act that pays off is act 1 if p *xor* q, act 2 if not.

We can look at our example in terms of logical inference. The receiver has—in a way—learned to infer p *xor* q from the premises p, *not*-q, its denial from the premises p, q, and so forth. The inferences are not just valid inferences, but also the *relevant* valid inferences for the task at hand. Receivers can learn to compute other truth functions and to perform other inferences in just the same way.

4. Error: Taking a Vote

So far, our senders have been infallible observers of the state of the world. They may not have seen everything, but what they think they have seen they have indeed seen. Senders' strategies so far have been based on the truth, if not always the whole truth. In the real world there is observational error.[4]

If there is imperfect observation, it may make sense to ask for a second or third opinion. Consider the most basic Lewis signaling game, with two equiprobable states, two signals and two acts, but with three senders. Each sender observes the state, but with some error—errors independent—and sends a signal to the receiver. Then the receiver chooses an act.

It is not possible for signals to carry perfect information about the state. Error is endemic to the model. It is not possible for a signaling system to assure that the receiver always gets it right. But it is possible for an equilibrium to minimize the effects of error. The senders can convey perfect information about their fallible observations, and the receiver can pool this information to make the best choice. The optimal receiver's strategy is then to take a vote. If the majority of senders "say" it is state one, then the receiver should do act one; if a majority of senders "say" it is state 2 then the receiver should do act 2. We could call this sort of equilibrium a "Condorcet signaling system." Taking a vote allows a significant improvement over the payoffs attainable with only one sender.

For example, with an error rate for observations of 10%, our receiver will have an error rate of less than 3%. Simulations of Roth–Erev learning for this example show individuals always

---

[4] Nowak and Krakauer 1999 consider a different kind of error, receiver's error in perceiving the signal. They suggest that minimizing this kind of error played an important role in the evolution of syntax.

converging to a Condorcet equilibrium.[5] With a few more senders the error rate can be driven very low, as the Marquis de Condorcet pointed out in 1785.[6]

Logic and information processing

When multiple senders convey different information to a receiver (or to multiple receivers) the receiver is confronted with a problem of information processing. How does one take all these inputs and fix on what to output—what to do? Logical inference is only part of this bigger problem of information processing. It is a problem routinely solved every second by our nervous system as floods of sensory information are filtered, integrated, and used to control conscious and unconscious actions. We have seen how a few rudiments of this process can emerge from simple adaptive dynamics.

Logic redux: Chrysippus' hunting dog

If we consider basic logic as information processing rather than as something living in Plato's ideal realm, the emergence of logic appears much less mysterious. Logic may be conscious or unconscious. There is no reason to think of it as the sole possession of humans. This way of looking at logic is not new. It has been debated since Hellenistic times. Consider Chrysippus' hunting dog.

According to Sextus Empiricus, Chrysippus tells the story of a dog that, not unlike my hypothetical vervets at the beginning of this chapter, performs a disjunctive syllogism:

---

[5] Simulations by Rory Smead, reported in supporting matter for Skyrms 2009.
[6] In his *Essay on the Application of Analysis to the Probability of Majority Decisions*, Condorcet assumes a jury decides a matter of fact by majority vote, probability that jurors are correct is greater than .5, and jurors' errors are independent. Then the probability of a correct decision approaches certainty as the size of the jury goes to infinity.

And according to Chrysippus, who shows special interest in irrational animals, the dog even shares in the far-famed "Dialectic." This person, at any rate, declares that the dog makes use of the fifth complex indemonstrable syllogism when, arriving at a spot where three ways meet, after smelling at the two roads by which the quarry did not pass, he rushes off at once by the third without stopping to smell. For, says the old writer, the dog implicitly reasons thus: The creature went either by this road, or by that, or by the other: but it did not go by this road or by that: therefore it went by the other.[7]

You could think of the dog's brain getting signals from his eyes and from his nose, and having to integrate the resulting pieces of information.

Chrysippus himself did not think that the dog reasoned, holding to the Stoic position that animals, unlike humans, do not have reason (*logos*). He held instead that the dog acts *as if* he could reason. He thus opposes the view of Sextus. This frames a debate that has come down through the history of philosophy[8]—Descartes on the side of the Stoics, Hume on the side of the skeptics.[9] Luciano Floridi recounts a report of a debate on the subject organized for King James I at Cambridge in 1614. The question of the debate was whether dogs could make syllogisms. John Preston took the skeptic position and Matthew Wreb the stoic side. King James concluded "that Wreb had to think better of his dogs or not so well of himself."[10] You will have your own opinion. I am with David Hume and King James.

[7] Sextus Empiricus, *Outlines of Pyrrhonism* ch. XIV.
[8] See Floridi 1997 for the detailed story.
[9] Hume 1793, Bk I Pt III Sec XVI.
[10] Mayor 1898, quoted in Floridi 1997.

12

Complex Signals and Compositionality

Humans are not restricted to one-word sentences, but rather can construct complex utterances whose content is a function of the content of their parts. This capability has sometimes been claimed to set man apart from beast. Such claims are somewhat overblown.[1] Birdsongs often string together in complex ways, and in some birds these are ways in which the content of the parts contributes to the content of the whole. Monkeys in the wild show some rudimentary steps in this direction. Domesticated apes, parrots, and dolphins have done more. Humans have gone much further down this road than other animals, but the use of complex signals is not unique to humans.

We try to understand the first step in this journey—the move from simple atomic signals to signals composed of parts. If one has little to communicate, simple signals may be perfectly adequate. But if one has a lot to say, complex signals introduce obvious economies. A lot can be communicated using combinations of a few basic parts. If it costs something to maintain a signal, there are obvious economies to be had by using complex signals. Martin Nowak and David Krakauer argue that complex signals may, in addition, increase the fidelity of information transmission, by preventing simple signals getting crowded together as the perceivable

---

[1] As we have seen in Chapter 2.

space of potential signals gets filled up.[2] By recombining parts, one can routinely construct new signals. Complex signals may make it easier to learn a signaling system, especially if the content of a complex signal is a function of the contents of its parts. Complex signals can facilitate information processing—as is evident from the development of formal logic. Complex signals can certainly be useful in many ways. It is not difficult to construct models where they confer an evolutionary advantage in a context where rich information exchange is important. We can suppose that if we have them they will confer a Darwinian advantage. But how could they arise in the first place?

There are contributions to the literature that address this question. John Batali investigates the emergence of complex signals in populations of neural nets.[3] Simon Kirby extends the model in a small population of interacting artificial agents.[4] These models assume structured mental meanings that are meant to be conveyed by the sender in the signal string, and structured meanings that the receiver gets from interpreting the signal string, and a way to compare sender's meaning to speaker's meaning to determine success or failure.[5] Structured meanings like <John, loves, Mary> could, in principle, be conveyed by one-word signals, but systems of structured signals are observed to evolve.

These are important contributions to the problem. Here, however, I want to start at an earlier point in the evolution of signaling. I am interested in how one might come to have—in the most primitive way—a complex signal composed of simple signals.

[2] See Nowak and Krakauer 1999.
[3] Batali 1998.
[4] Kirby 2000.
[5] As Kirby 2007 succinctly puts it:

Early models such as Batali 1998 and Kirby 2000 involved populations of individual computational agents. These agents were equipped with: explicit internal representations of their languages (e.g. grammars, connection weights, etc.); a set of meanings (provided by some world model) about which they wished to communicate; mechanisms for expressing signals for meanings using their linguistic representations; and algorithms for learning their language by observing meaning-signal pairs (e.g. grammar induction, back propagation, etc.).

And I would like to do this with the smallest departure possible from signaling models that have been previously examined in this book.

We have seen how a receiver can process different information from multiple senders. Multiple senders need not be different individuals, but could instead be the same individual at different times. A monkey who sees the grass move and sends the "leopard or snake" alarm call might run up a nearby tree and then be able to see that there is no leopard. It could then be able to send a signal to that effect. What is important is that there are separate pieces of information, not separate individuals sending them. The information processing problem faced by the receiver is exactly the same in both cases.

Let us revisit the *inventing the code* model from the last chapter. One sender observes whether the situation is up or down and sends the signal red or green. Another sender observes whether the state of the world is left or right and sends the signal yellow or blue. Interactions with a receiver who needs both pieces of information to make an optimal decision can lead to a complex signaling system. The receiver treats the juxtaposition of two signals as conjunction, which is simply to say that they are treated as two pieces of information to be integrated. In a community of individuals who are sometimes in one observational situation sometimes in another, this complex signaling system can become fixed.

If it is fixed, receivers have a fixed interpretation of pairs of signals. Suppose, for instance that the system is:

Red => Top
Green=> Bottom
Yellow=> Left
Blue => Right

In such a community, a sender who is well placed enough to observe that the state of the world is exactly <Bottom, Left> can communicate this by sending a complex signal consisting of green and yellow, in any order. This leads to a primitive signaling system that exhibits a simple kind of *compositionality*. The information in a complex signal is a function of the information in its parts. It is not so far from integration of information from separate signals to the integration of information from separate parts of a complex signal.

The next stage in the development of compositionality is sensitivity to order.

This is the key that opens the door to richer compositionality: subject–predicate or operator–sentence. But sensitivity to temporal order is something many organisms have already developed in responding to perceptual signals. The efficient frog reacts different- ly to *first fly left*, *next fly center* than to perceptual signals in the opposite order.

More generally, we can say that temporal pattern recognition is a fundamental mechanism for anticipating the future. In the second stage of compositionality, this general-purpose mechanism is re- cruited to allow more complex signaling systems. We see begin- nings of this process in bird calls.

Once we have sensitivity to order in complex signals, it is possible to have prototypes of sentential operators. Recall the "boom-boom" operator of Campbell's monkeys discussed in Chapter 2. The alarm call for a predator is prefaced by two low "boom" calls when the predator is distant and not an immediate danger. There is a basic signal, which is modified by what we would view as an operator. Much of the data on complex signals in the wild is quite recent. That is because investigators have looked for what isn't supposed to be there.

Some philosophers seem desperate to draw a line between hu- mans and other animals—I have never understood why. However that may be, the line isn't here. We already find rudiments of compositionality in animal signaling, and once we have this then the evolutionary advantages of compositional signaling systems that have been noted in the literature can come into play. Why then, haven't lots of animals developed language? Perhaps they don't have that much to say. Their signaling systems are adequate to their needs.

13

Networks II: Teamwork

Giant moray eels and groupers are both predators of fish in the Red Sea. Groupers take their prey in open water. Moray eels take theirs in crevices in the reef. Redouin Bshary, Andrea Hohner, Karim Ait-el-Djoudi, and Hans Fricke describe cooperative hunting between eels and groupers.[1] If a prey fish eludes a grouper by entering a crevice, the grouper may approach a moray eel, signal it using special head movements, and lead it to the fish's location. The eel will pursue it in the reef and either catch it or drive it out. If it comes out the grouper gets it. The proportion of times eel and grouper get fed is about equal, and cooperative hunts are more than twice as likely as solitary hunts to bag a prey.

Cooperative hunting within a species has been observed in lions, chimpanzees, dolphins, and hawks. Even the lowly bacterium *Myxococcus xanthus* engages in a kind of cooperative hunting, in which chemical signals are used to coordinate attack.[2] They swarm over prey microorganisms, excrete enzymes to digest them, and absorb the nutrients. Cooperative hunting is one example of teamwork in animals and men. So is cooperative defense, as when wildebeest form a protective circle with young in the center, or birds mob a predator. So are cooperative foraging, rearing of young, or building of communal habitation. Any multicelled organism is a marvel of teamwork.

---

[1] Bshary et al. 2006.
[2] Berleman et al. 2008.

In some teamwork problems, such as mobbing a predator or swarming prey, a uniform action by all members of the team produces the requisite effect. Others call for a more sophisticated teamwork, involving a division of labor and coordination of tasks.[3] Division of labor may involve morphological differentiation. We see this in various ways in the castes of insect societies, in cells and organs of the body, and even in differentiation of soma and spore in reproduction of *Myxococcus xanthus*.

In contrast, division of labor among morphologically similar individuals is central to human economic activity. But it is also found in many other species. Consider, however, group hunts of 3 or 4 lionesses in Etosha National Park, Namibia.[4] Two lionesses, the *wings*, attack a group of prey from either side, panicking them to run forward. They run right into one or two other lionesses, positioned as *centers*, who are waiting for them. This sort of hunting is highly successful. Variations on this kind of cooperative hunting with specialized roles have been observed in many other species.[5]

Bottle-nosed dolphins near Florida engage in group hunts where one individual acts as a *driver* and herds fish into a circle formed by the rest of the dolphins who act as *barrier*, preventing the fish from escaping.[6] Herding into a barrier is implemented in a different way by humpback whales. One whale swims in circles underwater blowing a "curtain" of bubbles. The other whales herd fish into this virtual trap from below and drive them up to the surface where all feed.

For many tasks the use of signals is crucial in establishing the coordination needed for effective teamwork. Teamwork may in some circumstances be achieved by a simple exchange of signals between equals. In other situations a good team may need a leader.

---

[3] Anderson and Franks 2001 require division of labor in their definition of teamwork.

[4] Stander 1992.

[5] Dugatkin 1997; Anderson and Franks 2001.

[6] Gazada et al. 2005.

Quorum-sensing revisited

In quorum-sensing by bacteria there are many senders and receivers, and each individual is both a sender and receiver. Each individual must judge the number (or intensity) of ambient signals, and take the appropriate action when the intensity is high enough. Signaling in the real process is incredibly complex both between cells and within cells, and very far from our toy models of signaling.

At the simplest level, nature chooses the number of individuals. Each individual continually sends out a low level of signal. Individuals can observe the intensity (or number in a discrete model) of ambient "I am here" signals. Thus, everyone signals everyone. Individuals either turn on genes to produce light or not—we don't ask how. The payoff depends on the number of bacteria producing light. If just a few do, the effort is wasted and the squid perhaps is eaten. If a lot do, the effort is rewarded. We assume a threshold of individuals below which the payoff is zero and above which it is one.

Assuming for the moment (and contrary to fact) that the sending strategy is fixed, bacteria need only to evolve a receiver's strategy that switches the lights on if the incoming number of signals is above the *quorum* level, and to switch them off if it is below that level. Pushing ahead with shameless oversimplification, receivers' payoffs are 1 if they all switch the lights on above the quorum and off below the quorum, and zero otherwise. At this level, the problem is related to that of "taking vote" that we considered earlier, but it is even simpler, since there is no alternative sender's strategy. Evolution, learning, or any reasonable adaptive dynamics will have no trouble learning it.

So everything would be easy if signals were discrete, payoffs were step functions, and bacteria could count. The world inside the light organ of the squid is much more complicated. The signal is a small diffusible molecule, and the number of such molecules would be too great for simple organisms to count, even if they could count. The signal input is more like a continuous variable than a discrete number (or rate) of signals received. The required output is binary—light or no light—or close to it. Transient fluc-tuations due to chance shouldn't cause useless flickering on and off. Nature is faced with designing a robust bi-stable switch which turns the lights on and off in approximate synchrony and at approximate-ly the optimal concentration of bacteria.

A fairly general way to do this, well known in engineering, is to use a positive feedback loop. An input—output function that would otherwise be linear is modified by feedback to produce a "switch" function with some "stickiness" to activation to resist noise. Suppose the optimal point for the light to switch on or off is a concentration x. If the lights are on, a little positive feedback keeps them on for concentrations a little below x. If the lights are off a little positive feedback keeps them off a little above x.

Quorum-sensing bacteria have discovered the positive feedback trick. The signaling molecule is an autoinducer. The more "I am here" messages you get, the more you send. From a game theory point of view, we now have gradations of sender strategies, where number of signals sent depends on number of signals received. The whole story is really much more complicated than this, involving multiple feedback loops.[7] The basic biochemistry implementing this strategy is different in gram-negative and gram-positive bacte-ria, but the basic idea is the same. The construction of a robust bi-stable switch using feedbacks is not only used in quorum-sensing bacteria, but is one of the basic motifs found throughout biological signaling systems.[8]

Homeostasis

Another ubiquitous example of teamwork is the coupling of send-er, receiver, and nature in a negative feedback loop to achieve homeostasis. Here is a maximally simplified model. Nature presents

[7] Goryachev et al. 2006.

[8] Alon 2006; Goryachev et al. 2006; Brandman and Meyer 2008.

one of three states to the sender: *too hot, too cold,* or *just right.* The sender chooses one of three messages to send. The receiver chooses one of three acts: *turn up the heat, turn down the heat, don't change it.* The receiver's acts modify the state in the obvious way:

ACT	OLD STATE		NEW STATE
Turn up	*Too Cold*	=>	*Just Right*
	Just Right	=>	*Too Hot*
	Too Hot	=>	*Too Hot*
Don't Change	*Too Cold*	=>	*Too Cold*
	Just Right	=>	*Just Right*
	Too Hot	=>	*Too Hot*
Turn Down	*Too Cold*	=>	*Too Cold*
	Just Right	=>	*Too Cold*
	Too Hot	=>	*Just Right*

Things stay put for a while, but exogenous shocks occasionally perturb the state. The optimal action for a state obviously is one that leaves the state being *just right.* We give this a positive payoff and all others zero payoff.

A signaling-system equilibrium is one which always leads to this optimal action.

It is no more difficult for adaptive dynamics to arrive at such a *homeostatic signaling system* than to learn the three-state, three-signal, three-act signaling systems of earlier chapters.

More complex homeostatic signaling systems occur throughout our bodies, such as the blood glucose regulatory system with the pancreas in the role of sender, the liver in the role of receiver, and the hormones glucagon and insulin in the role of signals. All these systems—regulation of fluid volume, blood ion concentrations, and the rest—require one or more sensors (senders), one or more effectors (receivers), and signals from the former to the latter.

Dialogue

So far, senders were presented with information and, at most, had to decide what to send.[9] Let us consider a more interactive situation in which receivers can ask for information and senders can seek it out. We can suppose that the sender's observational partition is not fixed. The sender can choose which observation to make. That is to say, she can choose which partition of states to observe. Suppose also, that the receiver's decision problem is not fixed. Nature chooses a decision problem to present to the receiver. Different sorts of information are relevant to different decision problems.[10] Knowing the actual element of partition A (the element that contains the actual state) may be relevant to decision problem 1, while knowing the actual element of partition B may be relevant to decision problem 2. This opens up the possibility of signaling dialogue, where information flows in two directions.

In the simplest sort of example, nature flips a coin and presents player 2 with one or another decision problem. Player 2 sends one of two signals to player 1. Player 1 selects one of two partitions of the state of nature to observe. Nature flips a coin and presents player 1 with the true state. Player 1 sends one of two signals to player 2. Player 2 chooses one of two acts.

Suppose that there are four states $\{S_1, S_2, S_3, S_4\}$, with alternative partitions:

$P_1 = \{\{S_1, S_2\}, \{S_3, S_4\}\}$, $P_2 = \{\{S_1, S_3\}, \{S_2, S_4\}\}$, as shown below:

P_1:

S_1	S_2
S_3	S_4

---

[9] "Decide" being perhaps metaphorical, since our agents may or may not be making conscious decisions.

[10] Compare van Rooy 2003, who argues that the pragmatics of decision can be used to disambiguate questions in such conversational contexts.

P2:

S1	S2
S3	S4

The two decision problems require choices in different act sets: {A1, A2} for the first decision problem and {A3, A4} for the second. Payoffs for the two decision problems are:

	Decision 1	Decision 1	Decision 2	Decision 2
	Act 1	Act 2	Act 3	Act 4
State 1	1	0	1	0
State 2	1	0	0	1
State 3	0	1	1	0
State 4	0	1	0	1

Player 2 has a signal set {R, G} and player 1 has a signal set {B, Y}. A strategy for player 2 now consists of three functions, one a sender strategy from {P1, P2} into {R,G}, one a receiver strategy from {B,Y} into {A1, A2}, one a receiver strategy from {B,Y} into {A3, A4}. In a signaling-system equilibrium each player always gets a payoff of one. The possibility of dialogue introduces a plasticity of signaling that is absent in fixed sender-receiver games. Signaling systems are strict, and evolutionarily stable as before.

Signaling systems can evolve in the dialogue interaction in isolation, but simulations show this process to be very slow. Evolution of a signaling system is much easier if we assume that some of its components have evolved in less complicated interactions. Player 1 may already have signaling systems in place for the two different observational partitions as a consequence of evolution in simple sender-receiver interactions. If so, the evolution of dialogue only requires that the second player signal the problem and the first choose what to observe. This is no more difficult than evolution of a signaling system in the original Lewis signaling game.

Team leader I

It is sometimes the case that a well-placed sender knows what needs to be done, and can send messages to receivers who can act, but that no one receiver can do everything that needs to be done. It may also be the case that success requires division of labor. Receivers need to be coordinated in performing different tasks.

Suppose, for instance, that there are two receivers and one sender. The sender observes one of four equiprobable states of the world and sends one of two signals to each receiver. The receivers must each choose between two acts, and the acts must be coordinated in a way determined by the state for all to get a payoff. We take payoffs for combinations of receivers' acts to be:

	<Act1, Act1>	<Act1, Act2>	<Act2, Act1>	<Act2, Act2>
State 1	1,1,1	0,0,0	0,0,0	0,0,0
State 2	0,0,0	1,1,1	0,0,0	0,0,0
State 3	0,0,0	0,0,0	1,1,1	0,0,0
State 4	0,0,0	0,0,0	0,0,0	1,1,1

We assume that the sender can distinguish members of the team, so sender's strategy maps states into ordered pairs of signals and a receiver's strategy maps her signal into her space of acts. Here the problem to be solved is a combination of one of communication and one of coordination. It is solved in a signaling system equilibrium, in which everyone always gets a payoff of one. A signaling-system equilibrium is again a strict equilibrium, and the unique strict equilibrium in the game. It is a strongly stable attractor in the replicator dynamics.

In the foregoing example, the two receivers can be thought of as playing a rather trivial two-person game, but the game is different in every state of the world. In state 1 the receivers are playing the game:

	Act1	Act2
Act1	1,1	0,0
Act2	0,0	0,0

They only get paid if they both do act 1.
    In state 2:

	Act1	Act2
Act1	0,0	1,1
Act2	0,0	0,0

In this state they only get paid if they coordinate on the first receiver doing act 1 and the second doing act 2. Likewise for the other two states. In a signaling system, *the sender tells the receivers what the game is* and the sender gets paid for that information.

Team leader II (correlated equilibrium)

The example can be varied in many ways by changing the embedded two-person games and their effect on the payoffs to the sender. At the other end of the spectrum, we can suppose that the embedded games are all the same. But now we choose a less trivial embedded game, one with multiple equilibria. Consider the Hawk-Dove game a standard model of resource competition.[11]

    The game goes by many aliases. In other quarters it is known as "Chicken" or as "Snowdrift game." With the different names go different stories. The story for "Chicken" is that two teenagers drive towards each other at high speed, and the first to swerve loses face and is called a "chicken." This usage has migrated from

---

[11] From Maynard Smith and Price 1973.

"Rebel without a Cause" to international relations. The "Snow-drift" story has quite a different flavor.[12] Two drivers approach a snowdrift blocking a road. Doves shovel and Hawks just stand and wait. In the "Hawk-Dove" story of evolutionary game theory, two individuals contest a resource. Hawk beats Dove for the resource but when two Hawks fight there is serious injury or death. If you meet a Hawk it is best to be a Dove; if you meet a Dove it is best to be a Hawk.

Different stories may be appropriate to different versions of the basic kind of payoff matrix. Here are payoffs for one kind of Hawk-Dove game:

	Hawk	Dove
Hawk	0,0	7,2.
Dove	2,7	6,6

There are two pure equilibria in this game: player 1 plays Hawk and player 2 Dove and the converse arrangement. But there is also a serious possibility of mis-coordination. If each player aims for his preferred equilibrium, they both play Hawk—each hoping to intimidate the other—and end up fighting.[13]

Conflict could be avoided if a third party could, in an acceptable way, tell them on each occasion who is to play Hawk and who is to play Dove. We add an appropriate sender. The sender observes one of three equiprobable states of the world. Each receiver plays Hawk upon receipt of signal 1 and reacts to signal 2 by playing Dove. In state 1 the sender directs signal 1 to row and signal 2 to column, in state 2 she reverses the signals, and in state 3 they both get signal 2. Row and column now end up playing <Hawk, Dove>, <Dove,

[12] Sugden 2005.
[13] They would be better off both playing Dove, but this would fall apart. If one player pays Dove, the other is better off playing Hawk.

Hawk>, and <Dove, Dove>, each ⅓ of the time. They both now have an average payoff of 5.

Is it too convenient to assume that the sender has three equiprobable states to observe? No, the sender can easily create them by rolling a die. Why should the sender do this? The two receivers can each *pay* the sender a commission—say 5% of their payoffs—for performing this service. It is now in the sender's interest to promote the total payoff of the receivers, and in the receivers' interests to employ the sender.

The third party is assisting the players in implementing a *correlated equilibrium* of the embedded game—a fundamental solution concept of game theory introduced and analyzed by Robert Aumann.[14] In this example (due to Aumann), the receivers even do better than if they had somehow learned to alternate between the two pure equilibria <Hawk, Dove> and <Dove, Hawk>. And they do much better than if they were just blundering around, getting into fights. This game invites all sorts of interesting variations.

I am sure that you have already thought of some.

How difficult is it for players to learn to correlate in our model situation? They face more challenges than individuals did in the simple situations with which we began the book. We no longer have pure common interest, but rather a complicated web of competing interests. Each of the receivers does best when he is the Hawk while the other is the Dove. The sender would do best if she could get the receivers to both always be Doves, but each would have an incentive to deviate from this arrangement.

Leader-follower

Our two leader-follower examples are bookends for a shelf of models. In the first model the problem is one of coordination. The leader identifies the operative game and sends that information

---

[14] Aumann 1974, 1987.

to the receivers. The receivers then naturally do the best thing. The sender tells the receivers *what the game is*. In the second example the problem is one of partial conflict. The game is fixed, but knowledge of the game does not give unambiguous guidance. The team leader tells receivers *what to do*. In real teams, both considerations may come into play. An effective team leader may transmit some, but not all, of the information at her disposal. She may seek additional information as required, combining dialogue with direction.

14

Learning to Network

We now suppose that, in one of the ways investigated in preceding chapters, individuals have learned to signal. Building on this basis, how can they learn to combine these signaling interactions to form signaling networks? This is the next question for a naturalistic theory of signaling. It is too large a question for a single chapter, or even a single book. Here I will give an introduction to this growing area of research. I hope that you will find the simple examples treated here interesting and suggestive.

The spirit of the enterprise is intended to be consonant with the rest of this book: start with the simplest and most naive forms of trial-and-error learning and see what they can do. If they fail to solve a problem, climb up the ladder of cognitive sophistication to see what it takes. We start in a somewhat roundabout way by noting the importance of ring structures of symbolic exchange in primitive societies.

Rings in primitive societies

In 1920, Bronislaw Malinowski published an article entitled "Kula" in *Man*, the journal of the Royal Anthropological Society. In it, he described the Kula Ring, later made famous

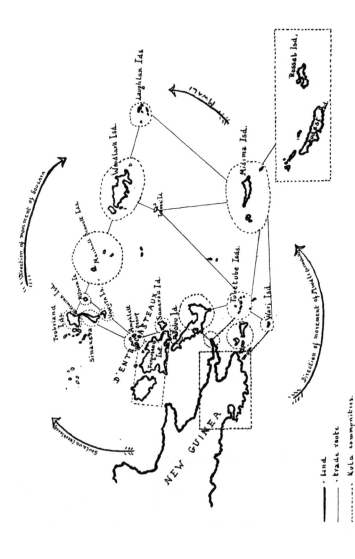

SKETCH MAP OF *KULA*

showing the area, trade routes and communities of the circular exchange. The dotted circles represent the *Kula*-communities, the dotted squares represent the districts indirectly affected by the *Kula*.

———— , Land

———— , trade route

·········· , Kula communities.

by his book *Argonauts of the Western Pacific*.[1] The ring, in Malinowski's words:

is based primarily upon the circulation of two articles of high value, but of no real use,—these are armshells made of the *Conus milleounctatus*, and necklets of red shell-discs, both intended for ornaments, but hardly ever used, even for this purpose. These two articles travel, in a manner to be described later in detail, on a circular route which covers many miles and extends over many islands. On this circuit, the necklaces travel in the direction of the clock hands and the armshells in the opposite direction. Both articles never stop for any length of time in the hands of any owner; they constantly move, constantly meeting and being exchanged.[2]

The necklaces and armshells have social, symbolic, and even magical value. They become more valuable as they circulate. Each subsequent owner adds to the history, power and value of an item.

Computer LAN rings

Before computer networking power was almost free, computers were sometimes organized in local area networks (LAN) with the structure of a ring. Each node passes information to an immediate neighbor in a specified direction—say clockwise—along the ring. Information then flows to all nodes around the ring. One disadvantage of a ring network is that it is not robust. If one node is disabled, information flow is disrupted. As insurance, sometimes ring networks also add counter-rotation, passing information to neighboring nodes in both clockwise and counter-clockwise directions, just like the Kula ring.

[1] Malinowski 1922.
[2] Malinowski 1920.

Some of the resemblance is misleading. Rotation combined with counter-rotation in the Kula has more to do with reciprocity than with robustness. But some resemblances may be significant. In particular, note that the good being passed on does not degrade as it passes along. The information is passed along reliably without appreciable decay in the computer LAN. The articles in the Kula ring also have a value that does not decay. It actually increases as they are passed along. This will prove to be an important consideration in game theoretic analysis of network formation.

The Bala–Goyal ring game

Venkatesh Bala and Sanjeev Goyal[3] introduce an informational network game in which a ring structure[4] has a special equilibrium status. Individuals get private information by observing the world. Each gets a different piece of information. Information is valuable. An individual can pay to connect to another and get her information. The individual who pays does not give any information; it only goes from payee to payer. The payer gets not only the information from private observations of those whom she pays, but also that which they have gotten from subscribing to others for their information. Information flows freely in this community, and without degradation, along the links so established. It flows in one direction, from payee to payer. We assume that information flow is fast, relative to any adjustment of the network structure.

If the cost of subscribing to someone's information is too high, then it won't pay for anyone to do it. But let's suppose that the cost of establishing a connection is less than the value of each piece of information. Then connections certainly make sense. We assume that any individual can make as many connections as she wishes. This model can be viewed as a game, with an individual's strategy

---

[3] Bala and Goyal 2000.
[4] They call it a "wheel."

being a decision of what connections to make. It could be none, all, or some. The game has multiple equilibria, but one is special. This is the ring (or circle). There is an example in figure 14.1.

The ring structure in this game is special in two ways. The first is that it is *strict*, the second that it is *efficient*. It is a strict equilibrium in that someone who unilaterally deviates from such a structure finds herself worse off. It is *Pareto efficient* in that there is no way to change it to make someone better off without making someone worse off. It is efficient in an even stronger sense. There is simply no way at all to make anyone better off. Everyone has the highest possible payoff that they could get in any network structure. The key to both these properties is that information flows freely around the ring, so that for the price of one connection a player gets all the information that there is.

Consider a player in such a ring who changes her strategy. She could establish additional links, in which case she pays more and

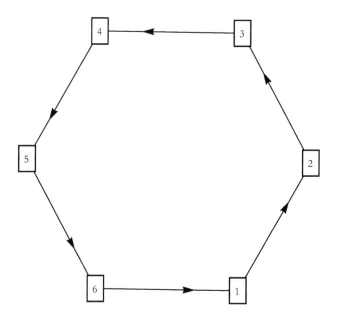

Figure 14.1: An information ring.

gets no more information. She could break her link, in which case she would forego the cost but get no information. She could break the link and establish one or more new ones, but every way to do that would deliver less than total information. Every deviation leaves her worst off. That is to say that the ring is a *strict* Nash equilibrium of the game.

Now let us ask a different question. Suppose that, starting from the ring, there is some lucky guy that everyone else would like to make better off, even if they have to sacrifice something to do it. There is nothing they can do! He is already getting all the information at the cost of one link. They cannot alter their links so as to give him more information, since he is already getting it all. Only he can avoid the cost of the link by breaking it—that is, not visiting anyone—but then he gets no information at all. The ring is strongly *efficient*.

Given these rather strong optimality properties of the ring, it is of interest to see if individuals playing this game can *learn* to form a signaling network with the structure of the ring. Experimental evidence is that in small group interactions with this game structure, individuals *do* spontaneously learn to form rings.[5] Do we have a plausible model of network dynamics that can account for this?[6]

A dynamic model of network formation

Robin Pemantle and I advanced a low rationality, trial-and-error model of network formation in 2000. The idea was the individuals start out by interacting at random and then learn *with whom to interact* by the kind of reinforcement learning with which we are familiar. Here is a simple model of the process. Each individual starts out with an urn with one ball of one color for each possible

[5] Callander and Plott 2005.

[6] The interested reader should consult modeling specifically directed at the Kula ring by Rolf Ziegler, which takes a somewhat different approach. See Ziegler 2007, 2008.

choice. Each day each individual chooses a ball from his urn, visits the indicated individual and has an interaction. Visits are always received. Visitor and visitee take numbers of balls of the partner's color proportional to the payoff received and add them to their respective urns. This is just learning whom to visit by the kind of reinforcement learning we have already studied in connection with learning to signal.

The Bala–Goyal game fits within this framework. We substitute altering connections for visiting, assume that information transfer is fast between changes in connections, and keep the reinforcement learning. Then we can justify the payoff function used by Bala and Goyal, and the equilibrium analysis is unchanged. However, network formation by reinforcement does not learn the ring. Rather extensive simulations show individuals maintaining probabilistic links with a variety of contacts. The structure is different each time. We just don't see the ring crystallizing out.[7]

There is no reason at all to believe that reinforcement learning should lead to an optimal solution to *every* problem. This is a situation where a little more sophistication in learning might be useful.

Simple inductive learning[8]

Suppose we move up to simple inductive learning. Individuals observe others' acts, form predictive probabilities by taking the average of their acts in the past, and choose a best response to those acts. If there are ties for best response, the players flip a coin. Instead of keeping track of rewards, individuals see how others' acts affect their payoffs, attempt to predict those acts in a simple way, and choose strategically. Now individuals often learn

---

[7] One might think of trying alternative forms of reinforcement learning, but—if anything—they tend to do worse.

[8] See Huttegger and Skyrms 2008.

the ring, but not always. It is still possible (but not likely) to get stuck in a sub-optimal state.

Slight modifications to this process, however, lead to uniform success. If players treat approximate ties as ties—for instance by computing expected payoff just to two decimal places—they always learn the ring network. The little bit of noise generated by approximate ties gets them out of the sub-optimal states. Here a little decrease in rationality helps. Can we reduce it more and still succeed?

Best response with inertia

Suppose we decrease our agent's sophistication a little more. Let's get rid of the inductive logic and just keep the best response. Most of the time players just keep on doing what they did last time, but once in a while someone wakes up and chooses a best response to what others did last time. She remembers the whole network structure as it was, assumes that no one else will change, and alters her network connections in the optimal way given that assumption. This is called *best response with inertia*. Bala and Goyal prove that this dynamics always learns the ring.

Low information—low rationality

The level of rationality has been lowered to rather modest levels. But our players still have to know some things in order to best-respond. They need to know the structure of the game: that is, how the actions of others affect their payoffs. And they need to know the existing network structure—what everyone did last time. There are circumstances in which these requirements are not plausible. Consider Malinowski's own observation about the Kula:

Yet it must be remembered that what appears to us an extensive, complicated, and yet well ordered institution is the outcome of so many doings and pursuits, carried on by savages, who have no laws or aims or charters definitively laid down. They have no knowledge of the *total outline* of any of their social structure. They know their own motives, know the purpose of individual actions and the rules which apply to them, but how, out of these, the whole collective institution shapes, this is beyond their mental range. Not even the most intelligent native has any clear idea of the Kula as a big, organized social construction . . . [9]

So we are led to ask whether there is a plausible low-information, low-rationality learning that succeeds here where reinforcement learning fails.

Probe and adjust

Suppose our individuals don't know the payoff structure of the game, and don't know what others have done. They only know what actions are open to them, what they have done, and what payoffs they got. We are almost back where we started. Again we suppose that individuals usually just keep doing what they are used to, but occasionally an individual chooses to explore. These choices are infrequent and independent, just like in the Bala–Goyal best-response dynamics. Call them *probes*. When an individual probes, she notes her payoff and compares it with what she is used to. If it is better she sticks with the probe strategy. If it is worse, she goes back to her old strategy. Ties are broken by a coin flip.

If probes are infrequent and independent, then it is very unlikely that multiple individuals probe at the same time, or subsequent times. Most individual probes occur in a context where everyone has been doing the same thing, a single individual tries an alternative while others stay the same, and the individual adjusts to the new strategy while others remain the same if it gives an increased payoff. If probes are very infrequent, then almost all probes will have this character. We can analyze a simplified process where they all do.

In the simplified process, nothing happens unless there is a probe. We can then focus on the states before and after a probe, with the

---

[9] Malinowski 1922.

transition probabilities being governed by the probabilities of probes (uniform) and their results. This gives us an embedded Markov chain. The rings are absorbing states, and the only ones. From any other state we can get to a ring with positive probability.[10] It follows that the embedded Markov process *always learns the ring*. That means that the original probe and adjust learning, learns the ring and stays close to it except for little fluctuations caused by ongoing probes. We have shown that it is possible for decentralized agents without global knowledge or strategic sophistication to learn the ring structure.[11]

Breakdown of the ring

Many primitive societies have ring exchanges of one sort or another. Susan McKinnon finds "male" and "female" gifts flowing in opposite directions in a ring structure in the Tanimbar islands.[12] Ceremonial exchange cycles are often accompanied with real economic exchange—with trade. They often interact with kinship. Exchange rings have been studied among aboriginals in Australia and Bantu in Africa. Some take place on land, so one cannot simply assume that the ring follows from the geography of a set of islands.

But ring structures are not to be found in every society. As societies become more complex, rings give way to other topologies. Claude Lévi-Strauss and others associate rings with egalitarian exchange, and the breakdown of the ring with the development of inegalitarian arrangements. Whether this generalization holds good or not, it is of interest to see why rings may not persist. In order to understand the breakdown of the ring, we might begin by

---

[10] This follows from the analysis given by Bala and Goyal for best response dynamics. [Theorem 3.1].

[11] This "Probe and Adjust" dynamics is similar to, but not identical with, the dynamics studied by Marden et al. 2009. For more on low rationality, payoff-based dynamics see Young 2009.

[12] McKinnon 1991.

investigating what happens when the assumptions behind the Bala–Goyal ring model are relaxed.

Relaxing assumptions

Information may decay (e.g. be corrupted by noise) as it passes form one node to another. This would be increasingly important when the ring grows large enough so that information passing through many links becomes highly degraded. Information flow may be two-way, rather than one-way. If so, costs of connection might be shared in various ways—perhaps with individuals bargaining over how the costs are shared. The items of information originating with different individuals might not be independent, or may not be equally valuable. Each of these variations, taken either separately or in combination, can make a difference. They are being actively explored in a growing literature.[13]

To get a little feeling for these factors, suppose we have a ring as in the Bala–Goyal game, and information flows without decay in two directions. Then any member of the ring would be happy to drop her connection, saving the connection cost and still getting all the information. The resultant topology is a line:

The individual at the foot of the line now free-rides on the others. He is not cut off because his information is worth more than the cost his neighbor pays to connect to him.

This arrangement is an equilibrium, in that no one can now do better by changing. But there are changes in which others do no worse. For instance, the individual at the head of the line might just as well break his connection and connect to someone else. He still pays the cost of one connection and gets all of the information.

[13] Bloch and Jackson 2007; Galeotti et al. 2006; Jackson 2008; Goyal 2007.

This is also an equilibrium. There are now lots of possible equilibria, and the population could drift among them.

But now suppose that one player, the center, pays to connect to each of the other players, and that is all. They are now in a star topology, as shown in figure 14.2.

Since the center is paying for all connections, it is called a *center-sponsored star*. Suppose that value of a unit of information is 1 and cost

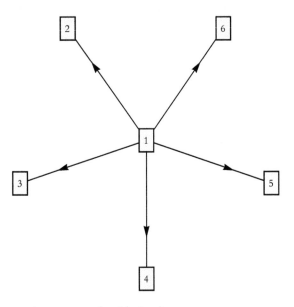

Figure 14.2: A star network with six players.

of establishing a link is 0.1. Then the center gets all the information, 6.0, less the cost of maintaining 5 links, for a net payoff of 5.5. Each of the other players free-rides on the links for a net payoff of 6.0.

You can verify that this is a strict Nash equilibrium. Any players would be worse off by deviating. If the center broke a link he would save 0.1 and lose 1.0. If a peripheral player made a link he would have to pay for it, whereas he now gets all the information without paying. If he broke a link he would simply lose information.

Bala and Goyal establish that in the case of two-way flow of information without decay, the center sponsored star is the unique

strict Nash equilibrium. (Providing the value of a unit of information is greater than the cost of making a link.) They also show that
the process of best response with inertia learns this star configuration
with probability one. For a low rationality, payoff-based approach,
we find that *probe and adjust* dynamics here approximates the star in
the same way that it approximated the ring in the earlier model.

Laboratory experiments, however, show that human subjects
perform quite differently in the two Bala–Goyal games. In experiments by Armin Falk and Michael Kosfeld[14] subjects learned the
ring quite well, but never learned the center-sponsored star. Explanations that have been floated focus on the difficulty of deciding
who would be in the center, and distaste for being the one player
who pays for all the connections.

Everything is changed if there is *information decay*. Suppose that
10% of the information is lost as it passes through a link. The value
of a bit of information is taken as 1 and the cost of connection as .1.

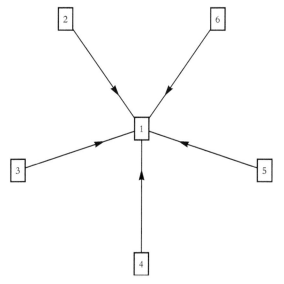

Figure 14.3: A star network with six players.

---

[14] Falk and Kosfeld 2003.

Now consider a *periphery-sponsored star*, where five players on the periphery pay to connect to the one in the center.

The lucky center pays no costs and is one link away from everyone else, for a payoff of 5.5. The players on the periphery, after cost, have a payoff of 5.04. This is a strict equilibrium. It isn't worth it for players on the periphery to pay .1 for a direct connection to one another to replace second-hand information that passed through the center (value .81) with first-hand information (value .9). They certainly don't want to break the connection to the center, who provides lots of second-hand information. His centrality is an asset. But note that with these values for cost of link formation and information decay, the center-sponsored star that we considered earlier is also a strict Nash equilibrium. If we raise the cost of connection up to 1.1, the center-sponsored star is not viable. The center would have to pay more for each connection than it is worth. But the periphery-sponsored star is viable if the players can get to it. Each peripheral player pays 1.1, which is well worth it given all the information she gets from the center.

Daniel Hojman and Adam Szeidl[15] have taken information decay further. They have constructed a class of models in which the *periphery-sponsored star* plays a special role. There is two-way flow of information, with strong decay in the value of information received, and with some "cut-off" distance such that information flowing from more distant sources is worthless. In the basic model, the initiator of a link bears its full costs, and all individuals are the same, although modifications of these assumptions are also explored.

In one realization of the basic model, each individual observes the state of the world with some error, errors being independent across individuals and error probabilities being the same for each individual. Increasing information exhibits decreasing returns—when you know with high probability the state, further confirmation is not worth so much. When observations are communicated

---

[15] Hojman and Szeidl 2008.

from one to another, further errors are introduced. For this basic model, Hojman and Szeidl prove that the unique Nash equilibrium of the network formation game is a *periphery-sponsored star*.

There are laboratory experiments on a game related to Hojman and Szeidel's model, but not quite the same. Seigfreid Berninghaus, Karl-Martin Ehrhart, Marion Ott, and Bodo Vogt.[16] consider a game where you get all your connection's information and if you paid for the link, you get all his connection's information as well, and that's all. There is no information decay per se, but the sharp cutoffs put a similar premium on short path length. Where the strict Nash equilibrium is a periphery-sponsored star, they find experimental subjects learning this star structure. However, when in such a star subjects sometimes fluctuate out and end up back in a star with a different individual as center.

It is remarkable how we now see breakdown of the ring and evolution of hierarchy, even though the population is perfectly homogeneous. Real populations are not homogeneous, of course, and some individuals have more valuable information than others. This may be because they are deeper thinkers, or better situated observers, or some combination of such factors. Hojman and Szeidl consider the effect of modifying their basic model to take account of such heterogeneity.

The equilibrium result is a population structure of interlinked stars, where the central figure of one star establishes a link to the central figure of another, either directly or through an intermediary. If there is a little noise operating, the central figures are the ones with the high-value information.

Conclusion

What are we to make of the parallels between dynamics of information networks and the networks of symbolic exchange

---

[16] Berninghaus et al. 2007.

discussed by anthropologists? I don't know the answer, but the question merits examination. The transition from rings to stars, linked stars, and more complicated structures is clearly of fundamental importance. The models discussed here already tell us very interesting things, but there is clearly a lot more to learn.

In this chapter, we introduced a low-rationality *probe and adjust* dynamics to approximate higher rationality learning in the basic Bala–Goyal models. Both best response dynamics and *probe and adjust* learned networks that reinforcement learning did not. Most of the dynamic models of network formation in the literature are either based on simple reinforcement learning,[17] or on some kind of best-response dynamics. The kind of best response with inertia used by Bala and Goyal is also used by other game theorists.[18] We would therefore like to know how far our results generalize.

It should be evident that, in general, *probe and adjust* learns a network structure if *best response with inertia* does. In the literature on *best response with inertia*, it is always assumed that responses are rare enough that we can assume that players don't respond simultaneously. This simpler idealized process is analyzed, just as we did with *probe and adjust*. If there is a best response move, then with positive probability *probe and adjust* will make it. Then suppose that, for every state, there is a positive probability best response path to an absorbing network state. It follows that, for every state, there is also a positive probability *probe and adjust* path to that state. If high rationality best response learns the network, the low rationality *probe and adjust* does so as well.[19]

[17] Skyrms and Pemantle 2000; Liggett and Rolles 2004; Pemantle and Skyrms 2004a, 2004b.

[18] For instance, Watts 2001; Jackson and Watts 2002, apply this to network formation.

[19] There are network games in which these dynamics do not learn the optimal network, such as the case of the Bala–Goyal peripheral sponsored star with high cost of connection discussed above. Starting without connections, any connection costs more than it is worth. It is only when the structure is in place that it pays everyone to maintain it.

Postscript

There is no mystery behind the emergence of signaling. Given favorable circumstances, adaptive processes can lead to spontaneous emergence of signaling systems. This is true for simple models of evolutionary dynamics based on random mutation and differential reproduction. It is just as true for various forms of trial-and-error learning. No special-purpose mental equipment is required. Spontaneous emergence of signaling is perfectly natural, and is to be expected when there is an advantage to be gained by transferring some information. Perfectly aligned interests between senders and receivers are by no means required, and deception is a real possibility.

There is no mystery about the meaning of signals. The object of primary interest is *information*. Signals naturally acquire information of a variety of types, and they can carry information both in and out of equilibrium. The Platonist's propositional notion of meaning is an abstraction from one kind of information in perfect equilibrium in an idealized signaling game.

Information flows throughout signaling networks. But there is a lot more going on than the simple transmission of information. Information is filtered, combined, and processed. Signaling networks perform computations and make inferences. Signals effect coordinated behavior between multiple actors—often for mutual benefit. The details of how this works in even the simplest natural signaling networks are amazingly complex.

But amid the rich scientific landscape, some recurrent patterns have emerged. These network motifs have been discovered empirically in a wide variety of biological networks. They are small network modules from which larger networks are constructed.[1] Ubiquitous motifs include filters, switches, feedback loops of various kinds, and structures that implement simple inference. Understanding how these evolved, and how nature puts them together, is a challenge for naturalistic philosophy.

[1] See Milo et al. 2002; Wolf and Arkin 2003; Alon 2006, 2007.

References

Aldous, D. (1985) "Exchangeability and Related Topics." In *L'École d'été de probabilités de Saint-Flour, XIII–1983* 1–198. Berlin: Springer.

Alon, U. (2006) *An Introduction to Systems Biology: Design Principles and Biological Circuits.* Chapman and Hall.

Alon, U. (2007) "Network Motifs: Theory and Experimental Approaches." *Nature* 8: 450–461.

Anderson, C. and N. R. Franks (2001) "Teams in Animal Societies." *Behavioral Ecology* 12: 534–540.

Argiento, R., R. Pemantle, B. Skyrms, and S. Volkov (2009) "Learning to Signal: Analysis of a Micro-Level Reinforcement Model." *Stochastic Processes and their Applications* 119: 373–390.

Aristotle *Historia Animalium* Book IX.

Aristotle *Physics* Book II.

Asher, N., I. Sher and M. Williams (2001) "Game Theoretical Foundations for Gricean Constraints." In *Proceedings of the Thirteenth Amsterdam Colloquium.* Amsterdam: IILC.

Aumann, R. (1987) "Subjectivity and Correlation in Randomized Strategies." *Journal of Mathematical Economics* 1: 67–96.

Aumann, R. (1987) "Correlated Equilibrium as an Expression of Bayesian Rationality." *Econometrica* 55: 1–18.

Bala, V. and S. Goya (2000) "A Noncooperative Model of Network Formation." *Econometrica* 68: 1181–1231.

Barnes, J. (2001) *Early Greek Philosophy.* 2nd edn. London: Penguin.

Barnes, J. (1982) *The Presocratic Philosophers.* London: Routledge.

Barrett, J. A. (2006) "Numerical Simulations of the Lewis Signaling Game: Learning Strategies, Pooling Equilibria, and the Evolution of Grammar." Working Paper MBS06–09. University of California, Irvine.

Barrett, J. A. (2007a) "The Evolution of Coding in Signaling Games." *Theory and Decision.* DOI: 10.1007/s11238–007–9064–0.

Barrett, J. A. (2007b) "Dynamic Partitioning and the Conventionality of Kinds." *Philosophy of Science* 74: 527–546.

Barrett, J. A. and K. Zollman (2007) "The Role of Forgetting in the Evolution and Learning of Language." preprint.

Batali, J. (1998) "Computational Simulations of the Evolution of Grammar." In *Approaches to the Evolution of Language: Social and Cognitive Bases*, ed. J. R. Hurford et al. Cambridge: Cambridge University Press.

Bauer, W. D. and U. Mathesius (2004) "Plant Responses to Bacterial Quorum-Sensing Signals." *Current Opinion in Plant Biology* 7: 429–433.

Beggs, A. (2005) "On the Convergence of Reinforcement Learning." *Journal of Economic Theory* 122: 1–36.

Benaim, M. (1999) "Dynamics of Stochastic Approximation Algorithms." In *Seminaire de Probabilites* 33. Berlin: Springer Verlag.

Benaim, M., S. J. Shreiber, and P. Tarres (2004) "Generalized Urn Models of Evolutionary Processes." *Annals of Applied Probability* 14: 1455–1478.

Bereby-Meyer, Y. and I. Erev (1998) "On Learning How to be a Successful Loser: A Comparison of Alternative Abstractions of Learning Processes in the Loss Domain." *Journal of Mathematical Psychology* 42: 266–286.

Berg, R. M. van den (2008) *Proclus' Commentary on the Cratylus in Context*. Leiden: Brill.

Bergstrom, T. (2002) "Evolution of Social Behavior: Individual and Group Selection Models." *Journal of Economic Perspectives* 16: 231–238.

Bergstrom, C. T. and M. Lachmann (1998) "Signaling Among Relatives III. Talk is Cheap." *Proceedings of the National Academy of Sciences USA* 95: 5200–5105.

Berleman, J. E., J. Scott, T. Chumley, and J. R. Kirby (2008) "Predataxis Behavior in *Myxococcus Xanthus*." *Proceedings of the National Academy of Sciences USA* 105: 17127–17132.

Berninghaus, S., K.-M. Ehrhart, M. Ott, and B. Vogt (2007) "Evolution of Networks–an Experimental Analysis." *Journal of Evolutionary Economics* 17: 317–347.

Bickerton, D. (1990) *Language and Species*. Chicago: University of Chicago Press.

Björnerstedt, J. and J. Weibull (1995) "Nash Equilibrium and Evolution by Imitation." In K. Arrow et al. (eds.), 155–71, *The Rational Foundations of Economic Behavior*. New York: Macmillan.

Bloch, F. and M. Jackson (2007) "The Formation of Networks with Transfers among Players." *Journal of Economic Theory* 133: 83–110.

Bloch, F. and B. Dutta (2009) "Communication Networks with Endogenous Link Strength." *Games and Economic Behavior* 66: 39–56.

Blume, A. (2000) "Coordination and Learning with a Partial Language." *Journal of Economic Theory* 95: 1–36.

Blume, A., D. DeJong, Y.-G. Kim, and G. B. Sprinkle (1998) "Experimental Evidence on the Evolution of the Meaning of Messages in Sender-Receiver Games." *American Economic Review* 88: 1323–1340.

Blume, A., D. DeJong, Y.-G. Kim, and G. B. Sprinkle (2001) "Evolution of Communication with Partial Common Interest." *Games and Economic Behavior* 37: 79–120.

Blume, A., D. DeJong, G. Neumann, N. E. Savin (2002) "Learning and Communication in Sender-Receiver Games: An Econometric Investigation." *Journal of Applied Econometrics* 17: 225–247.

Borgers, T. and R. Sarin (1997) "Learning through Reinforcement and the Replicator Dynamics." *Journal of Economic Theory* 74: 235–265.

Borgers, T. and R. Sarin (2000) "Naive Reinforcement Learning with Endogenous Aspirations." *International Economic Review* 41: 921–950.

Brandman, O. and T. Meyer (2008) "Feedback Loops Shape Cellular Signals in Space and Time." *Science* 322: 390–395.

Brentano, F. (1874) *Psychology from an Empirical Standpoint*. London: Routledge.

Brown, G. W. (1951) "Iterative Solutions of Games by Fictitious Play." In *Activity Analysis of Production and Allocation*, ed. T. C. Koopmans. New York: Wiley.

Bshary, R., A. Hohner, K. Ait-el-Djoudi, and H. Fricke (2006) "Interspecific Communicative and Coordinated Hunting between Groupers and Giant Moray Eels in the Red Sea." *PLoS Biology* 4:2393–2398 4:e431, DOI:10:1371/journal.pbio.0040431.

Bush, R. and F. Mosteller (1955) *Stochastic Models of Learning*. John Wiley & Sons: New York.

Callander, S. and C. R. Plott (2005) "Principles of Network Development and Evolution: An Experimental Study." *Journal of Public Economics* 89: 1469–1495.

Camerer, C. and T-H. Ho (1999) "Experience Weighted Attraction Learning in Normal Form Games." *Econometrica* 67: 827–874.

Campbell, G. (2003) *Lucretius on Creation and Evolution*. Oxford: Oxford University Press.

Charrier, I. and C. B. Sturdy (2005) "Call-Based Species Recognition in the Black-Capped Chickadees." *Behavioural Processes* 70: 271–281.

Cheney, D. and R. Seyfarth (1990) *How Monkeys See the World: Inside the Mind of Another Species*. Chicago: University of Chicago Press.

Chomsky, N. (1957) *Syntactic Structures*. The Hague: Mouton.

Cross, J. G. (1973) "A Stochastic Learning Model of Economic Behavior." *Quarterly Journal of Economics* 87: 239–266.

Crawford, V. and J. Sobel (1982) "Strategic Information Transmission." *Econometrica* 50: 1431–1451.

Cubitt, R. and R. Sugden (2003) "Common Knowledge, Salience and Convention: A Philosophical Reconstruction of David Lewis' Game Theory." *Economics and Philosophy* 19:175–210.

Dante *The Divine Comedy of Dante Alighieri*. Trans. H. F. Cary, ed. Jim Manis. PSU Electronic Classics, <http://www2.hn.psu.edu/faculty/jmanis/dante/comedy.pdf>.

De Morgan, A. (1838) *An Essay on Probabilities and their Application to Life Contingencies and Insurance Offices*. London: Longman.

Donaldson, M. C., M. Lachmann, and C. T. Bergstrom (2007) "The Evolution of Functionally Referential Meaning in a Structured World." *Journal of Theoretical Biology* 246: 225–233.

Dretske, F. (1981) *Knowledge and the Flow of Information*. Cambridge: MIT Press.

Dugatkin, L. A. (1997) *Cooperation Among Animals: An Evolutionary Perspective*. Oxford: Oxford University Press.

Dyer, F. C. and T. D. Seeley (1991) "Dance Dialects and Foraging Range in three Asian Honey Bee Species." *Behavioral Ecology and Sociobiology* 28: 227–233.

Edwards, W. (1961) "Probability Learning in 1000 Trials." *Journal of Experimental Psychology* 62: 385–394.

Erev, I. and E. Haruvy (2005) "On the Potential Uses and Current Limitations of Data-Driven Learning Models." *Journal of Mathematical Psychology* 49: 357–371.

Erev, I. and A. Roth (1998) "Predicting How People Play Games: Reinforcement Learning in Experimental Games with Unique Mixed-Strategy Equilibria." *American Economic Review* 88: 848–881.

Estes, W. K. (1950) "Toward a Statistical Theory of Learning." *Psychological Review* 57: 94–107.

Evans, C. S., C. L. Evans and P. Marler (1994) "On the Meaning of Alarm Calls: Functional Reference in an Avian Vocal System." *Animal Behavior* 73: 23–38.

Falk, A. and M. Kosfeld (2003) "It's All About Connections: Evidence on Network Formation." IEW Working Paper 146. University of Zurich.

Feltovich, N. (2000) "Reinforcement-Based vs. Belief-Based Learning Models in Experimental Asymmetric-Information Games." *Econometrica* 68: 605–641.

Flache, A. and M. Macy (2002) "Stochastic Collusion and the Power Law of Learning." *Journal of Conflict Resolution* 46: 629–653.

Floridi, L. (1997) "Skepticism, Animal Rationality, and the Fortune of Chrysippus' Dog." *Archiv für Geschichte der Philosophie* 79: 27–57.

Frede, D. and B. Inwood (2005) *Language and Learning: Philosophy of Language in the Hellenistic Age.* Cambridge: Cambridge University Press.

Fudenberg, D. and D. Levine (1998) *A Theory of Learning in Games.* Cambridge, MA: MIT Press.

Galeotti, A. and S. Goyal (2008) "The Law of the Few." Working paper, University of Essex.

Galeotti, A., S. Goyal, and J. Kamphorst (2006) "Network Formation with Heterogeneous Players." *Games and Economic Behavior* 54: 353–372.

Gazda, S., R. C. Connor, R. K. Edgar, and F. Cox (2005) "A Division of Labour with Role Specialization in Group-hunting Bottlenose Dolphins (*Tursiops truncatus*) off Cedar Key, Florida." *Proceedings of the Royal Society B* 272: 135–140.

Gentner, T. Q., K. M. Fenn, D. Margoliash, and H. C. Nusbaum (2006) "Recursive Syntactic Pattern Learning by Songbirds." *Nature* 440: 1204–1207.

Gettier, E. (1963) "Is Justified True Belief Knowledge?" *Analysis* 23:121–123.

Godfrey-Smith, P. (1989) "Misinformation." *Canadian Journal of Philosophy* 19: 522–550.

Godfrey-Smith, P. (2000a) "On the Theoretical Role of Genetic Coding." *Philosophy of Science* 67: 26–44.

Godfrey-Smith, P. (2000b) "Information, Arbitrariness and Selection: Comments on Maynard-Smith." *Philosophy of Science* 67: 202–207.

Good, I. J. (1950) *Probability and the Weighing of Evidence*. London: Charles Griffin.

Good, I. J. (1983) *Good Thinking: The Foundations of Probability and its Applications*. Minneapolis: University of Minnesota Press.

Gould, J. L. (1975) "Honey Bee Recruitment: the Dance Language Controversy." *Science* 189: 685–693.

Gould S. J., and N. Eldredge (1977) "Punctuated Equilibria: The Tempo and Mode of Evolution reconsidered." *Paleobiology* 3: 115–151.

Goryachev, A. B., D. J. Toh, and T. Lee (2006) "Systems Analysis of a Quorum Sensing Network: Design Constraints Imposed by the Functional Requirements, Network Topology and Kinetic Constants." *BioSystems* 83: 178–187.

Goyal, S. (2007) *Connections: An Introduction to the Economics of Networks*. Princeton: Princeton University Press.

Green, E. and T. Maegner (1998) "Red Squirrels, *Tamiasciurus hudsonicus*, Produce Predator-Class Specific Alarm Calls." *Animal Behavior* 55: 511–518.

Grice, H. P. (1957) "Meaning." *Philosophical Review* 66: 377–388.

Grice, H. P. (1975) "Logic and Conversation." In *Syntax and Semantics*, vol. 3, ed. P. Cole and J. L. Morgan, 41–58. New York: Academic Press.

Grice, H. P. (1989) *Studies in the Way of Words*. Cambridge, MA: Harvard University Press.

Griffiths, P. E. (2001) "Genetic Information: A Metaphor in Search of a Theory." *Philosophy of Science* 68: 394–412.

Grim, P., P. St. Denis, and T. Kokalis (2002) "Learning to Communicate: The Emergence of Signaling in Spatialized Arrays of Neural Nets." *Adaptive Behavior* 10: 45–70.

Grim, P., T. Kokalis, A. Alai-Tafti, A., and N. Kilb (2000) "Evolution of Communication in Perfect and Imperfect Worlds." *World Futures: The Journal of General Evolution* 56: 179–197.

Grim, P., T. Kokalis, A. Alai-Tafti, N. Kilb, and P. St. Denis (2004) "Making Meaning Happen." *Journal of Experimental and Theoretical Artificial Intelligence* 16: 209–243.

Gyger, M., P. Marler, and R. Pickert (1987) "Semantics of an Avian Alarm Call System: The Male Domestic Fowl, *Gallus Domesticus*." *Behavior* 102: 15–20.

Hadeler, K. P. (1981) "Stable Polymorphisms in a Selection Model with Mutation." *SIAM Journal of Applied Mathematics* 41: 1–7.

Hailman, J., M. Ficken, and R. Ficken (1985) "The 'Chick-a-dee' calls of *Parus atricapillus*." *Semiotica* 56: 191–224.

Hamilton, W. D. (1963) "The Evolution of Altruistic Behavior." *American Naturalist* 97: 354–356.

Hamilton, W. D. (1964) "The Genetical Evolution of Social Behavior I and II." *Journal of Theoretical Biology* 7: 1–52.

Hamilton, W. D. (1967) "Extraordinary Sex Ratios." *Science* 156: 477–488.

Hamilton, W. D. (1971) "Selection of Selfish and Altruistic Behavior in Some Extreme Models." In *Man and Beast*, ed. J. F. Eisenberg and W. S. Dillon, 59–91. Washington, D.C.: Smithsonian Institution Press.

Hamilton, W. D. (1995) *Narrow Roads of Gene Land*. vol. 1: *Evolution of Social Behavior*. New York: W. H. Freeman.

Harley, C. B. (1981) "Learning the Evolutionarily Stable Strategy." *Journal of Theoretical Biology* 89: 611–633.

Harms, W. F. (2004) *Information and Meaning in Evolutionary Processes*. Cambridge: Cambridge University Press.

Hauert, C., S. De Monte, J. Hofbauer, and K. Sigmund (2002) "Volunteering as Red Queen Mechanism for Cooperation in Public Goods Games." *Science* 296, 1129–1132.

Hauser, M. D. (1988) "How Infant Vervet Monkeys Learn to Recognize Starling Alarm Calls: The Role of Experience." *Behavior* 105: 187–201.

Hauser, M. D. (1997) *The Evolution of Communication*. Cambridge, MA: MIT Press.

Hauser, M. D., N. Chomsky, and W. T. Fitch (2002) "The Faculty of Language: What is it, Who has it, and How did it Evolve." *Science* 298: 1569–1579.

Hebb, D. (1949) *The Organization of Behavior*. New York: Wiley.

Herman, L. M., D. G. Richards, and J. P. Wolz (1984) "Comprehension of Sentences by Bottle-Nosed Dolphins." *Cognition* 16: 129–219.

Herrnstein, R. J. (1961) "Relative and Absolute Strength of Response as a Function of Frequency of Reinforcement." *Journal of Experimental Analysis of Behavior* 4: 267–272.

Herrnstein, R. J. (1970) "On the Law of Effect." *Journal of the Experimental Analysis of Behavior* 13: 243–266.

Ho, T. H., X. Wang, and C. Camerer (2008) "Individual differences in EWA Learning with Partial Payoff Information." *The Economic Journal* 118: 37–59.

Hofbauer, J. (1985) "The Selection-Mutation Equation." *Journal of Mathematical Biology.* 23: 41–53.

Hofbauer, J. and S. Huttegger (2008) "Feasibility of Communication in Binary Signaling Games." *Journal of Theoretical Biology* 254: 843–849.

Hofbauer, J. and K. Sigmund (1998) *Evolutionary Games and Population Dynamics.* Cambridge: Cambridge University Press.

Hojman, D. A. and A. Szeidl (2008) "Core and Periphery in Networks." *Journal of Economic Theory.* 139: 295–309.

Holland, J. (1975) *Natural and Artificial Systems.* Ann Arbor, Michigan: University of Michigan Press.

Hölldobler, B. and E. O. Wilson (1990) *The Ants.* Cambridge, MA: Belknap.

Hoppe, F. M. (1984) "Pólya-like Urns and the Ewens Sampling Formula." *Journal of Mathematical Biology* 20: 91–94.

Hopkins, E. (2002) "Two Competing Models about How People Learn in Games." *Econometrica* 70, 2141–2166.

Hopkins, E. and M. Posch (2005) "Attainability of Boundary Points under Reinforcement Learning." *Games and Economic Behavior* 53: 110–125.

Hume, D. (1739) *A Treatise of Human Nature.* London: John Noon.

Hurford, J. (1989) "Biological Evolution of the Saussurean Sign as a Component of the Language Acquisition Device." *Lingua* 77: 187–222.

Huttegger, S. (2007a) "Evolution and the Explanation of Meaning." *Philosophy of Science* 74: 1–27.

Huttegger, S. (2007b) "Evolutionary Explanations of Indicatives and Imperatives." *Erkenntnis* 66: 409–436.

Huttegger, S. (2007c) "Robustness in Signaling Games." *Philosophy of Science* 74: 839–847.

Huttegger, S. and B. Skyrms (2008) "Emergence of Information Transfer by Inductive Learning." *Studia Logica* 89: 237–256.

Huttegger, S., B. Skyrms, R. Smead, and K. Zollman (2009) "Evolutionary Dynamics of Lewis Signaling Games: Signaling Systems vs. Partial Pooling." *Synthese.* DOI: 10.1007/s11229-009-9477-0

Izquierdo, L., D. Izquierdo, N. Gotts, and J. G. Polhill (2007) "Transient and Asymptotic Dynamics of Reinforcement Learning in Games." *Games and Economic Behavior* 61: 259–276.

Jackendoff, R. (2002) *Foundations of Language*. Oxford: Oxford University Press.

Jackson, M. (2008) *Social and Economic Networks*. Princeton: Princeton University Press.

Jackson, M. and A. Watts (2002) "On the Formation of Interaction Networks in Social Coordination Games." *Games and Economic Behavior* 41: 265–291.

Kaiser, D. (2004) "Signaling in Myxobacteria." *Annual Review of Microbiology* 58: 75–98.

Kant, I. (1965) [1785] *Fundamental Principles of the Metaphysics of Morals*. Trans. Thomas Kingsmill Abbott Project Gutenberg. 10 edn. London: Longmans Green.

Kavanaugh, M. (1980) "Invasion of the Forest by an African Savannah Monkey: Behavioral Adaptations." *Behavior* 73: 239–60.

Kirby, S. (2000) "Syntax without Natural Selection: How Compositionality Emerges from Vocabulary in a Population of Learners." In *The Evolutionary Emergence of Language*, ed. C. Knight, 303–323. Cambridge: Cambridge University Press.

Kirby, S. (2007) "The Evolution of Meaning-Space Structure through Iterated Learning." In *Emergence of Communication and Language*, ed. C. Lyon et al., 253–268. Berlin: Springer Verlag.

Kirchhof, J. and K. Hammerschmidt (2006) "Functionally referential Alarm Calls in Tamarins (Saguinus fuscicollis and Saguinus mystax)– Evidence from Playback Experiments." *Ethology* 112: 346–354.

Kirkup, B. C. and M. A. Riley (2004) "Antibiotic-Mediated Antagonism Leads to a Bacterial Game of Rock-Paper-Scissors *in vivo*." *Nature* 428: 412–414.

Komarova, N. and P. Niyogi (2004) "Optimizing the Mutual Intelligibility of Linguistic Agents in a Shared World." *Artificial Intelligence* 154: 1–42.

Komarova, N., P. Niyogi, and M. Nowak (2001) "The Evolutionary Dynamics of Grammar Acquisition." *Journal of Theoretical Biology* 209: 43–59.

Kosfeld, M. (2004) "Economic Networks in the Laboratory." *Review of Network Economics* 3: 20–41.

Kirchhof, J. and K. Hammerschmidt (2007) "Functionally Referential Alarm Calls in Tamarins (*Saguinis fusicollis* and *Saguinis mystax*.)—Evidence from Playback Experiments." *Ethology* 112: 346–354.

Kullback, S. and R. A. Leibler (1951) "On Information and Sufficiency." *Annals of Mathematical Statistics* 22: 79–86.

Kullback, S. (1959) *Information Theory and Statistics*. New York: John Wiley.

Lévi-Strauss, C. (1969) *The Elementary Structures of Kinship*. Boston: Beacon Press.

Lewis, D. K. (1969) *Convention*. Cambridge, MA: Harvard University Press.

Liggett, T. M. and S. Rolles (2004) "An Infinite Stochastic Model of Social Network Formation." *Stochastic Processes and their Applications* 113: 65–80.

Lindley, D. (1956) "On a Measure of the Information Provided by an Experiment." *The Annals of Mathematical Statistics* 27: 986–1005.

Lloyd, J. E. (1965) "Aggressive Mimicry in Photuris: Firefly Femmes Fatales." *Science* 149: 653–654.

Lloyd, J. E. (1975) "Aggressive Mimicry in Fireflies: Signal Repertoires of Femmes Fatales." *Science* 187: 452–453.

Luce, R. D. (1959) *Individual Choice Behavior*. John Wiley & Sons: New York.

Macedonia, J. M. (1990) "What is Communicated in the Antipredator Calls of Lemurs: Evidence from Antipredator Call Playbacks to Ringtailed and Ruffed Lemurs." *Ethology* 86: 177–190.

McKinnon, S. (1991) *From a Shattered Sun*. Madison: University of Wisconsin Press.

Macy, M. (1991) "Learning to Cooperate: Stochastic and Tacit Collusion in Financial Exchange." *American Journal of Sociology* 97: 808–843.

Macy, M. and A. Flache (2002) "Learning Dynamics in Social Dilemmas." *Proceedings of the National Academy of Sciences of the USA* 99: 7229–7236.

Malinowski, B. (1920) "Kula: The Circulating Exchange of Valuables in the Archipelagoes of Eastern New Guinea." *MAN* 20: 97–105.

Malinowski, B. (1922) *Argonauts of the Western Pacific*. New York: Dutton.

Manser, M., R. M. Seyfarth, and D. Cheney (2002) "Suricate Alarm Calls Signal Predator Class and Urgency." *Trends in Cognitive Science* 6: 55–57.

Marden, J. P., H. P. Young, G. Arslan, and J. S. Shamma (2009) "Payoff-based dynamics for Multiplayer Weakly Acyclic Games." *SIAM Journal on Control and Optimization* 48: 373–396.

Marler, P. (1999) "On Innateness: Are Sparrow Songs 'Learned' or 'Innate.'" In *The Design of Animal Communication*, ed. Marc Hauser and Mark Konishi. Cambridge, MA: MIT Press.

Maynard Smith, J. and G. R. Price (1973) "The Logic of Animal Conflict." *Nature* 246: 15–18.

Maynard Smith, J. and G. A. Parker (1976) "The Logic of Asymmetric Contests." *Animal Behaviour* 24: 159–175.

Maynard Smith, J. (1982) *Evolution and the Theory of Games*. Cambridge: Cambridge University Press.

Maynard Smith, J. (2000) "The Concept of Information in Biology." *Philosophy of Science* 67: 177–194.

Maynard Smith, J. and D. Harper (2003) *Animal Signals*. Oxford: Oxford University Press.

Mayor, J. (1898) "King James I On the Reasoning Faculty in Dogs." *The Classical Review* 12: 93–96.

McGregor, P. (2005) *Animal Communication Networks*. Cambridge University Press: Cambridge.

Merin, A. (1999) "Information, Relevance, and Social Decisionmaking: Some Principles and Results of Decision-Theoretic Semantics." In L. Moss, J. Ginzburg, M. de Rijke (eds.), 179–221, *Logic, Language, and Computation*, vol. 2. Stanford: CSLI.

Miller, M. B. and B. Bassler (2001) "Quorum Sensing In Bacteria." *Annual Review of Microbiology* 55: 165–199.

Millikan, R. G. (1984) *Language, Thought and Other Biological Categories*. Cambridge, MA: MIT Press.

Milo, R., S. Shen-Orr, S. Itzkovitz, N. Kashtan, D. Chklovskii, and U. Alon (2002) "Network Motifs: Simple Building Blocks of Complex Networks." *Science* 298: 824–827.

Nowak, M. A. and D. Krakauer (1999) "The Evolution of Language." *Proceedings of the National Academy of Sciences of the USA* 96: 8028–8033.

Nowak, M., J. Plotkin, and D. Krakauer (1999) "The Evolutionary Language Game." *Journal of Theoretical Biology* 200: 147–162.

Nowak, M. and K. Sigmund (1993) "A Strategy of Win-stay, Lose-shift that Outperforms Tit-for-tat in the Prisoner's Dilemma Game." *Nature* 364: 56–58.

Oliphant, M. (1994) "The Dilemma of Saussurean Communication." *Biosystems* 37: 31–38.

Othmer, H. G. and A. Stevens (1997) "Aggregation, Blow Up and Collapse: The ABC's of Taxis in Reinforced Random Walks." *SIAM Journal on Applied Mathematics* 57: 1044–1081.

Papineau, D. (1984) "Representation and Explanation." *Philosophy of Science* 51: 550–72.

Papineau, D. (1987) *Reality and Representation*. Oxford: Blackwell.

Parikh, P. (2001) *The Use of Language*. Stanford: CSLI.

Pawlowitsch, C. (2008) "Why Evolution Does Not Always Lead to an Optimal Signaling System." *Games and Economic Behavior* 63: 203–226.

Pemantle, R. (1990) "Nonconvergence to Unstable Points in Urn Models and Stochastic Approximations." *Annals of Probability* 18: 698–712.

Pemantle, R. (2007) "A Survey of Random Processes with Reinforcement." *Probability Surveys* 4: 1–79.

Pemantle, R. and B. Skyrms (2004a) "Network Formation by Reinforcement Learning: The Long and the Medium Run." *Mathematical Social Sciences* 48: 315–327.

Pemantle, R. and B. Skyrms (2004b) "Time to Absorption in Discounted Reinforcement Models" *Stochastic Processes and Their Applications* 109: 1–12.

Pinker, S., and R. Jackendoff (2005) "The Faculty of Language: What's Special About It?" *Cognition* 95: 201–236.

Pitman, J. (1995) "Exchangeable and Partially Exchangeable Random Partitions." *Probability Theory and Related Fields* 102: 145–158.

Proclus. (2007) *On Plato Cratylus*. Trans. Brian Duvick. London: Duckworth.

Quine, W. V. O. (1936) "Truth by Convention." In *Philosophical Essays for A. N. Whitehead*, ed. O. H. Lee. 90–124.

Quine, W. V. O. (1969) "Epistemology Naturalized." In *Ontological Relativity and Other Essays*. New York: Columbia University Press.

Rainey, H. J., K. Zuberbühler, and P. J. B. Slater (2004) "Hornbills Can Distinguish between Primate Alarm Calls." *Proceedings of the Royal Society of London B* 271: 755–759.

J. Riley, R. U. Greggers, A. D. Smith, D. R. Reynolds, and R. Menzel (2005) "The Flight Paths of Honeybees Recruited by the Waggle Dance." *Nature* 435: 205–207.

Robbins, H. (1952) "Some Aspects of the Sequential Design of Experiments." *Bulletin of the American Mathematical Society* 58: 527–535.

van Rooy, Robert. (2003) "Questioning to Resolve Decision Problems." *Linguistics and Philosophy* 26:727–763.

Roth, A. and I. Erev (1995) "Learning in Extensive Form Games: Experimental Data and Simple Dynamical Models in the Intermediate Term." *Games and Economic Behavior* 8: 164–212.

Russell, B. (1921) *The Analysis of Mind*. (Lecture X) London: George Allen and Unwin.

Russell, B. (1948) *Human Knowledge, Its Scope and Limits*. New York: Simon and Schuster.

Salmon, T. C. (2001) "An Evaluation of Econometric Models of Adaptive Learning." *Econometrica* 1597–1628.

Savage-Rumbaugh, S., K. McDonald, R. A. Sevkic, W. D., Hopkins, and E. Rupert (1986) "Spontaneous Symbol Acquisition and Communicative Use by Pygmy-Chimpanzees *(Pan Paniscus)*" *Journal of Experimental Psychology: General* 114: 211–235.

Savage-Rumbaugh, S. and R. Lewin (1994) *Kanzi: An Ape at the Brink of the Human Mind*. New York: Wiley.

Schauder, S. and B. Bassler (2001) "The Languages of Bacteria." *Genes and Development* 15: 1468–1480.

Schlag, K. (1998) "Why Imitate and If So, How? A Bounded Rational Approach to Many Armed Bandits." *Journal of Economic Theory* 78, 130–156.

Schreiber, Sebastian J. (2001) "Urn Models, Replicator Processes, and Random Genetic Drift", *SIAM Journal on Applied Mathematics*, 61.6: 2148–2167.

Schultz, W. (2004) "Neural Coding of Basic Reward Terms of Animal Learning Theory, Game Theory, Microeconomics and Behavioural Ecology." *Current Opinion in Neurobiology* 14:139–147.

Searcy, W. A. and S. Nowicki (2005) *The Evolution of Animal Communication: Reliability and Deception in Signaling Systems*. Princeton: Princeton University Press.

Sedley, D. (1998) *Lucretius and the Transformation of Greek Wisdom*. Cambridge: Cambridge University Press.

Sedley, D. (2003a) *Plato's Cratylus*. Cambridge: Cambridge University Press.

Sedley, D. (2003b) *"Lucretius and the New Empedocles."* Leeds International Classical Studies 2.4: 1–12.

Selten, R. and W. Massimo (2007) "The Emergence of Simple Languages in an Experimental Coordination Game." *Proceedings of the National Academy of Sciences of the USA* 104: 7361–7366.

Seyfarth, R. M. and D. L. Cheney (1990) "The Assessment by Vervet Monkeys of Their Own and Other Species' Alarm Calls." *Animal Behavior* 40: 754–764.

Shannon, C. (1948) "A Mathematical Theory of Communication." *The Bell System Mathematical Journal* 27: 379–423, 623–656.

Shannon, C. and W. Weaver (1949) *The Mathematical Theory of Communication*. Urbana: University of Illinois Press.

Shreiber, S. (2001) "Urn Models, Replicator Processes and Random Genetic Drift." *SIAM Journal on Applied Mathematics* 61: 2148–2167.

Sinervo, B. and C. M. Lively (1996) "The Rock-Paper-Scissors Game and the Evolution of Alternative Male Strategies." *Nature* 380: 240–243.

Skyrms, B. (1996) *Evolution of the Social Contract*. Cambridge: Cambridge University Press.

Skyrms, B. (1998) "Salience and Symmetry-Breaking in the Evolution of Convention." *Law and Philosophy* 17: 411–418.

Skyrms, B. (1999) "Stability and Explanatory Significance of Some Simple Evolutionary Models." *Philosophy of Science* 67: 94–113.

Skyrms, B. (2000) "Evolution of Inference." In *Dynamics of Human and Primate Societies*, ed. Tim Kohler and George Gumerman, 77–88. New York: Oxford University Press.

Skyrms, B. (2004) *The Stag Hunt and the Evolution of Social Structure*. Cambridge: Cambridge University Press.

Skyrms, B. (2005) "Dynamics of Conformist Bias." *Monist* 88: 260–269.

Skyrms, B. (2007) "Dynamic Networks and the Stag Hunt: Some Robustness Considerations." *Biological Theory* 2: 7–9.

Skyrms, B. (2009) "Evolution of Signaling Systems with Multiple Senders and Receivers." *Philosophical Transactions of the Royal Society B* doi:10.1098/rstb.2008.0258, 364: 771–779.

Skyrms, B. (2009) "Presidential Address: Signals." *Philosophy of Science* 75:489–500.

Skyrms, B. and R. Pemantle (2000) "A Dynamic Model of Social Network Formation." *Proceedings of the National Academy of Sciences of the USA*. 97: 9340–9346

Skyrms, B. and S. L. Zabell (forthcoming) "Inventing New Signals."

Slobodchikoff, C. N., J. Kiriazis, C. Fischer, and E. Creef (1991) "Semantic Information Distinguishing Individual Predators in the Alarm Calls of Gunnison's Prairie Dogs." *Animal Behaviour* 42: 713–719.

Smith, A. (1983) [1761] *Considerations Concerning the First Formation of Languages*. Reprinted in *Lectures on Rhetoric and Belles Lettres*, ed. J. C. Bryce. Oxford: Oxford University Press.

Snowdon, C. T. (1990) "Language Capacities of Nonhuman Animals." *Yearbook of Physical Anthropology* 33: 215–243.

Sorabji, R. (1993) *Animal Minds and Human Morals: The Origins of the Western Debate*. Ithaca: Cornell University Press.

Stander, P. E. (1990s) "Cooperative Hunting in Lions: The Role of the Individual." *Behavioral Ecology and Sociobiology* 29: 445–454.

Stanford, P. K. (2007) *Exceeding Our Grasp*. Oxford: Oxford University Press.

Steels, L. (1997) "The Synthetic Modeling of Language Origins." *Evolution of Communication* 1: 1–35.

Steels, L. (1998) "The Origins of Syntax in Visually Grounded Robotic Agents." *Artificial Intelligence* 103: 133–156.

Sterelny, K. (2000) "The 'Genetic Program' Program: A Commentary on Maynard-Smith on Information in Biology." *Philosophy of Science* 67: 195–201.

Sterelny, K. (2003) *Thought in a Hostile World: The Evolution of Human Cognition*. Oxford: Blackwell.

Struhsaker, T. T. (1967) "Auditory Communication among Vervet Monkeys *Cercopithecus aethiops*." In *Social Communication among Primates*, ed. S.A. Altmann, 281–324. Chicago: University of Chicago Press.

Sugden, R. (2005) *The Economics of Rights, Co-operation and Welfare* (Basingstoke: Macmillan).

Suppes, P. and R. Atkinson (1960) *Markov Learning Models for Multiperson Interactions*. Palo Alto, CA: Stanford University Press.

Taga, M. E. and B. L. Bassler (2003) "Chemical Communication Among Bacteria." *Proceedings of the National Academy of Sciences of the USA* 100 Suppl. 2, 14549–14554.

Taylor, P. and L. Jonker (1978) "Evolutionarily Stable Strategies and Game Dynamics." *Mathematical Biosciences* 40, 145–156.

Tempelton, C., E. Greene and K. Davis (2005) "Allometry of Alarm Calls: Black-Capped Chickadees Encode Information about Predator Size." *Science* 308: 1934–1937.

Thorndike, E. L. (1911) *Animal Intelligence.* New York: Macmillan.

Thorndike, E. L. (1927) "The Law of Effect." *American Journal of Psychology* 39: 212–222.

Trapa, P. and M. Nowak (2000) "Nash Equilibria for an Evolutionary Language Game." *Journal of Mathematical Biology* 41: 172–188.

Vencl, F., B. J. Blasko, and A. D. Carlson (1994) "Flash Behavior of Female Photuris Versicolor Fireflies in Simulated Courtship and Predatory Dialogues." *Journal of Insect Behavior* 7: 843–858.

Verlinsky, A. (2005) "Epicurus and his Predecessors on the Origin of Language." In Frede and Inwood 56–100.

Vanderschraaf, P. (1998) "Knowledge, Equilibrium and Convention." *Erkenntnis* 49: 337–369.

Vitruvius (1960) *The Ten Books of Architecture* Bk. 2 Ch. 1. Tr. Morris Hicky Morgan New York: Dover.

von Frisch, K. (1967) *The Dance Language and Orientation of the Bees.* Cambridge, MA: Harvard University Press.

von Neumann, J. and Morgenstern, O. (1944) *Theory of Games and Economic Behavior.* Princeton: Princeton University Press.

Wagner, E. (2009) "Communication and Structured Correlation." *Erkenntnis* doi 10.1007/s10670–009–9157–y.

Wärneryd, K. (1993) "Cheap Talk, Coordination, and Evolutionary Stability." *Games and Economic Behavior* 5: 532–546.

Watts, A. (2001) "A Dynamic Model of Network Formation." *Games and Economic Behavior* 34: 331–341.

Weber, R. and C. Camerer (2003) "Cultural Conflict and Merger Failure: An Experimental Approach." *Management Science* 49: 400–415.

Wei, L. and S. Durham (1978) "The Randomized Play-the-winner Rule in Medical Trials." *Journal of the American Statistical Association* 73: 840–843.

Weibull, J. (1995) *Evolutionary Game Theory.* Cambridge, MA: MIT Press.

Wolf, D. M. and A. P. Arkin (2003) "Motifs, Modules and Games in Bacteria." *Current Opinion in Microbiology* 6: 125–134.

Young, H. P. (2009) "Learning by Trial and Error." *Games and Economic Behavior* 65: 626–643.

Zabell, S. L. (1992) "Predicting the Unpredictable." *Synthese* 90: 205–232.

Zabell, S. L. (2005) *Symmetry and Its Discontents: Essays in the History of Inductive Probability*. Cambridge: Cambridge University Press.

Zeeman, E. C. (1980) "Population Dynamics from Game Theory." In *Global Theory of Dynamical Systems*, Springer Lecture Notes on Mathematics 819.

Ziegler, R. (2007) *The Kula Ring of Bronislaw Malinowski: A Simulation Model of the Co-Evolution of an Economic and Ceremonial Exchange System*. Munich: C. H. Beck Verlag.

Zeigler, R. (2008) "What Makes the Kula Go Round?" *Social Networks* 30: 107–126.

Zollman, K. (2005) "Talking to Neighbors: The Evolution of Regional Meaning." *Philosophy of Science* 72: 69–85.

Zuberbühler, K. (2000) "Referential Labeling in Diana Monkeys." *Animal Behavior* 59: 917–927.

Zuberbühler, K. (2001) "Predator-Specific Alarm Calls in Campbell's Monkeys, *Cercopithecus Campbelli*." *Behavioral Ecology and Sociobiology* 50: 414–422.

Zuberbühler, K. (2002) "A Syntactic Rule in Forest Monkey Communication." *Animal Behavior* 63: 293–299.

Zuidema, W. (2003) "Optimal Communication in a Noisy and Heterogeneous Environment." In *Proceedings Lecture Notes on Artificial Intelligence* v. 2801 Berlin: Springer 553–563.

Index